Praise for
Leah Carey's work:

"Leah Carey is a bright light in the field of self-empowerment and writing as a healing art. With *Transforming Your Body Image* she has created a step-by-step guide that empowers the user to discover their own unique beauty - a change that begins with the mind, not the waistline."

Iyanla Vanzant
Author of *Peace from Broken Pieces* and
One Day My Soul Just Opened Up

❧ ❧

"Leah Carey is a very talented visionary."

Jodi Picoult
Best-selling author of over 20 books, including *My Sister's Keeper*

❧ ❧

"Truthfully, choosing to read [*Transforming Your Body Image*] may be one of the most pivotal moments in my life. ... I promise you, the book is so fabulous and HONEST - which is a hugely important factor - that you can't go wrong. The truly amazing part is working your way through, from front to back, and realizing by the end that all of the fears and concerns and hindrances that you held within yourself were not only unnecessary, but terribly harmful to your well-being."

Samantha Lunger
Reviewer at *SweepTight.com*

❧ ❧

"Rather than encouraging a "just think positive" attitude, Carey's *Bosom Buddies* are a powerful example of what it means to examine the dark fears that come with a cancer diagnosis and come out the other side.

Dr. Joseph O'Donnell
Editor-In-Chief, *Journal of Cancer Education*

❧ ❧

"I was able to see my own anger, fear, and self-pity mirrored back to me from the pages of my writing, and I've let go of so much."

Workshop participant

"I love how you get us to do exercises so we can experience what you are telling us."

Workshop participant

ᔧ ᔨ

"You've created a safe environment for me to bring the fear, hurt, and anger from the depths of my soul out into the light, where I could take a look from a different perspective."

Workshop participant

ᔧ ᔨ

"Leah, you taught me how to remember my past. Even my most insignificant remembrances are incidents of my life that I do not ever want to forget. Thank you for helping me to realize that. Thank you for helping me to find the pathway to writing my memories."

Workshop participant

ᔧ ᔨ

"Leah is a wonderful facilitator. She is adept at overseeing the group and putting everyone at ease."

Workshop participant

ᔧ ᔨ

"This is important necessary work. More and more people should take part in this. It is healing, it challenges and creates linkages in the community and friendships to hold back the encroaching dark."

Workshop participant

ᔧ ᔨ

"You created a safe, welcoming place. I gained perspective and joy for the little gifts."

Workshop participant

ᔧ ᔨ

"Your program was perfect for reconnecting all of us to a deeper level in ourselves, our souls and heart. You are a wonderful teacher, guide and witness to all our needs and strengths."

Workshop participant

TRANSFORMING YOUR BODY IMAGE

A Journey To Loving Your Body

with

Leah Carey

For the two Big Mamas in my life

Sybil Carey birthed me into this world and has showered me with love. Every step of the way, she has supported my hopes and dreams.

Iyanla Vanzant taught me to birth my own self back into the world when I thought I was beyond help. She taught me to believe in my hopes and dreams again.

To my Mom and my Mama, I love you and I am so grateful to have been in your care. It is thanks to you that I now give birth to this manifestation of my hopes and dreams.

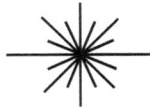

The 40-day process in this book is intended as a tool for self-discovery and self-empowerment. It is not a substitute for medical care and is not intended as a means of self-diagnosis or treatment of physical or mental conditions. I encourage you to take responsibility for your well-being, which includes regular visits to your health-care providers.

Welcome to
the process of
Transforming Yourself!

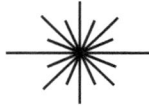

You will find that in just 20 minutes a day, you can experience a major shift in your thinking and feeling about your body.

The purpose of this program is to help you be at peace with your body. It is NOT a weight loss tool. **While weight loss may be a pleasant side effect, do not let it be the measure of your success.** Learning to love your body is its own success.

My philosophy is that it's not about fixing anything that's wrong with you. Instead, it's about figuring out what's already right and building from there.

Quick Start Guide

Each day, read the prompt for the day in the journal.

Write about the day's topic for 20 minutes or 2 pages (or longer, if you wish). If you're a prolific writer, use extra paper and keep it in a companion folder or notebook.

Read the thought for the day.

If you miss a day, don't worry! Pick up the next day where you left off.

You don't have to believe right now that it will work. Just give yourself 20 minutes a day and let yourself be amazed!

Do I Have 20 Minutes A Day?

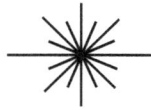

This is a question I often hear from clients: *how could I possibly spare 20 minutes in my already overcrowded, hectic day?* I know that most of us are scheduled within a hair's breadth of insanity these days, and there are so many things vying for our attention - work, family, email, cell phones, etc. Carving out 20 minutes a day from that perspective seems impossible.

So let's reframe the question: *How much time do you spend each day worrying about how you look?*

Do you spend 20 minutes in the morning poring over your closet, rejecting multiple outfits because you think they won't look good? How much time do you spend over the course of your day wondering if other people are looking at you and judging you? Do you think it approaches 20 minutes? Using my own experience as a guide, I'd wager that it's probably closer to a couple of hours a day...but the time is spread out amongst so many other things that we tend to forget about it.

Do you spend 20 minutes a day worrying about what you're going to eat/not eat/should eat/shouldn't eat...and then eating all the wrong things anyway and stressing about *that*?

I've been there. It's a painful way to live, and it's incredibly abusive to yourself. What if you used that 20 minutes a day in a more positive way and reaped the rewards of reclaimed time? You'll eliminate stress and feel better in the process!

The 40-Day Process

Traditionally, the number 40 represents a period of time in which a great change can occur. You'll find examples throughout the Bible, mythology, and folklore. It is often represented as a time of testing, purification, or enlightenment.

This process is structured as a 40-day cycle in order to tap into that archetypal symbolism to help you experience a period of growth and renewal.

"Fat and Ugly"

Kids can be cruel, but families can be even crueler.

The other kids in school told me I was ugly; it was my father who told me I was fat.

When I was a kid, I looked like a stick figure – long skinny arms, long skinny legs, and long skinny braid – but I don't even remember having that body because I never once thought about it. I know that by 4th grade, there were girls in my class who were already on diets, while my focus was on Nancy Drew's latest mystery and finding the next elusive piece to put in that week's jigsaw puzzle.

My attention didn't turn to my body until one night in 7th grade when my father told me that I was getting fat. I'd been on my junior high school cheerleading team, but I quit almost immediately because suddenly I was too ashamed to be seen in the short little skirt and form-fitting top. A friend asked me to join the basketball team, but those shorts were even skimpier than the cheerleading skirt, so I didn't even try out - even though I really wanted to.*

---

*It can be tempting to think of my father as the bad guy in this story, but that would be beside the point. Given the body-obsessed culture we live in, if I hadn't heard these words from him, I'm sure they would have come from someone else. The problem wasn't who said the words, or even what was said, but how my brain acted on them. No matter how mean he was, it could only affect me if I believed him. That doesn't mean that what my father said was okay, but it does mean that he's not to blame for what I did with what I heard.

My father started making "helpful" comments about my body more and more often, including the one that haunts me to this day: "You won't get a date if you don't have pretty legs." I began wearing huge baggy sweaters all the time to hide what I was sure was a disgusting and slovenly body. Just at the time that I was becoming aware of my body as a physical and sexual entity, I also became aware that I was fat. Too fat for anyone to love, including my own father.

The irony of all of this is that when I look at pictures from junior high and high school – *I wasn't fat at all!!!* I didn't have a perfectly flat stomach or gorgeous legs, but I had an attractively proportioned body – a body I would love to have today. Of course, if I could go back and reclaim that body, I hope that I'd dress better and have a better haircut!

I became increasingly self-conscious and horrified with my body as I entered the world of professional musical theatre. As a stage manager, I would sit in a rehearsal room all day with dancers – some of the most perfectly formed specimens of humanity on the earth. Rehearsal rooms are traditionally lined with mirrors; so whenever I stood up to walk across the room, I would see myself standing next to their tall, lithe, graceful bodies, and I'd feel like an elephant.

I became convinced that I was the "fat" girl that the "skinny" girls hung out with to make them look even skinnier and prettier. Getting dressed every day was an ordeal – nothing looked good, nothing felt good, and it seemed pointless to even try. Any time that I was with other people while I was eating, I was certain that they were thinking, "Look at what she's eating! No wonder she's so fat and ugly!"

It didn't matter what anyone said to me. If someone told me I looked pretty, I thought they were making fun and laughing at me behind my back. When someone said to me, "You have such a great smile," I imagined that inside their heads they were finishing the sentence "...but your thighs are HUGE!"

I bet that you are reading this because you have lived some version of this story yourself. The good news is that feeling better ultimately wasn't about changing my body, it was about changing my MIND.

In January 2007, I stood in a group healing circle of more than 40 women and said what I wholeheartedly believed to be the truth: "I am FAT and UGLY."

That day there was a teacher in the room who helped me to shift my perspective just enough to start moving on the right track. She said to me, "Do you have to pay extra to get on the bus because you're fat and ugly? Do you have to pay extra on your taxes because you're fat and ugly? If God created you as fat and ugly, that's His business. Let Him take care of your fat ugliness. You concentrate on being the best fat and ugly person you can be!" **Wow!** Those words made a serious impression on me. They got my attention, and that blunt message was exactly what I needed to hear.

Those words helped me to begin shifting my perspective from worrying about what everyone else thought when they looked at me, to thinking about how I could better care for my own body. For me, it was no longer about losing weight, but about honoring my body and treating it well.

As a result, I began to release the weight...and I didn't even notice. I didn't realize that I had dropped 15 pounds until other people started commenting on it. I was focused on my health, not my weight.

As long as I keep my focus on being healthy, my self-image is not tied to my weight. My weight still fluctuates, but it's not the end of the world because I'm busy being the ***best*** "fat and ugly" person I can be!

That is the power of a changed perspective. It was not an overnight change, but it was a powerful change that has stuck.

My hope for you is that whatever your story is, you'll find your own change of perspective through this process.

Get the Most Out of Your Process

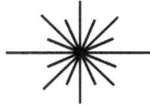

The writing prompts have been put in an order that facilitates a gradual process of looking inward.

Some prompts may not apply to you. WRITE ANYWAY! If the prompt asks about your father figure and you didn't have one, you might consider how not having a father figure affected your body image. Whatever you do, don't let this stop you from writing!

Address all of the questions, even if you feel that the question asks about something you've already dealt with. There's always a deeper level that can be addressed.

However, if there's a prompt that you absolutely can't answer, move on. Don't let one day's prompt stop you from continuing to move forward!

Be honest with yourself! It's not uncommon for someone to want to be so "spiritual" and "feel okay" that they will give the answers that they think are "right" and that sound the best. But that only perpetuates the myths and stories that you've already been telling yourself - and if you're doing this program, you already know that those haven't been working for you. You are only writing for yourself in this process, so take a risk and be really honest with yourself.

Bypass the first "easy" answer to the prompts and look more deeply for the real answer. The results can be startling, because *the shortest path to feeling better tomorrow is telling the truth about how you feel today.*

There will probably be days when you find something inside yourself that you didn't expect. You might remember things you had put away in a deep pocket of your mind. You might laugh; you might cry; you might feel like pounding on a pillow for a while. All of those things are okay. Tell at least one person who you trust that you're beginning this process so that you can call on them if there's a day when you need a hand to hold, a shoulder to cry on, or an ear to listen.

Allow yourself to feel bad if that's what comes up. Sadness, grief, and anger are all positive emotions *if* we acknowledge them, because they show us where something is ready to be healed. They're only a problem if we stuff them down and refuse to look at them.

Sometimes when we're going through a healing process, old habits can rear their ugly heads. For instance, when I began changing the way that I ate, some old behaviors reappeared. I suddenly started acting like a teenager with my mother again - whining, snapping, and being a general pain in the butt. I didn't know to expect that, so it was pretty disturbing for a few days and we both wondered what was going on. If some old behaviors start to appear (even ones that you worked hard to get rid of), it's okay. Your system is probably saying, "What the *&#$ do you think you're doing? We were comfortable doing things the old way!!" But when those thoughts and behaviors resurface, you're clearing and healing them, so keep with it and trust in yourself and your mind's ability to heal.

When thoughts, beliefs, and emotions stay bottled up in our heads, they can drive us batty with their repetitive, cyclical, fear-mongering nature. Study after scientific study has shown that getting those thoughts out on paper helps make them more manageable because they now have definition. It is easier to combat the monster that you can see than the monster that keeps changing form in the darkness of your mind.

If you have a friend who is also dealing with body image issues, invite them to work through this process at the same time so that you can encourage each other. There is more information on working with a partner near the end of these instructions.

Thought for the Day

There is an affirmation, message, or thought that will support you throughout each of the 40 days.

When you finish your writing, read the message for the day. Some days you may choose to carry the thought with you; other days you may read it and put it aside. Their purpose is to support you through your day.

Other Ideas to Support Yourself

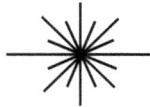

᚜   Find a quiet space to sit with your journal each day for 20 minutes. Make a ritual for yourself – for instance, if you're an early-morning riser, take advantage of that quiet time to write. If you enjoy an afternoon cup of tea, that would be a great time to sit and write. Perhaps you'd like to sit and write by a nearby brook or pond after dinner. Whatever it is, set aside a special 20 minutes for yourself each day as your sacred time to TRANSFORM YOURSELF.

᚜   Light a candle before you start writing each day.

᚜   Ask your angels/guides/protectors to be with you while you're writing.

᚜   At the end of each writing session, take a moment to summarize (in writing) the major revelation or thought that surfaced that day. This can help you focus today and provide a useful review of the highlights of your experience later.

᚜   If your daily highlight is particularly uplifting or thought-provoking, put it on an index card and carry it with you for the day so you can refer to it.

᚜   If at any point you get scared or overwhelmed, reach out for support. Ask for a hug. Read what you've written to someone else so that they can give you moral support. Share what you've learned about yourself with a friend. You don't have to do this alone!

∽ On the other hand, if there are people in your life who you think might not encourage you in your effort to TRANSFORM YOURSELF, don't share it with them. Part of this process is learning how to honor yourself, and that includes not allowing others to dishonor you.

※

You are worth your own time and effort. If you feel a little fragile sometimes, it's okay. Be gentle with yourself and know that healing takes time and is ALWAYS worth the effort.

The activity of this process takes just 20 minutes a day, but you may find the process is with you throughout your day. That's good! Embrace the process!

REMEMBER
**You'll get as much out of this
as you put into it!!**

Working with a Partner

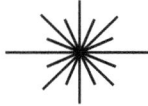

You may find that partnering with a friend provides wonderful structure and encouragement. Here are some thoughts on how to make this a great experience for both of you:

❧ Make sure you each have a copy of the book before you start! Because this journal is set up for you to write directly into the pages, you won't want to share a copy.

❧ Make an appointment to talk at least once a week. Share your thoughts, breakthroughs, challenges, and anything else that has come up.

❧ Holding each other accountable for the commitments you have made to yourselves is a very loving act. You may want to check in with each other briefly by phone or email each day to confirm that you have done the writing for the day. This will aid you both in staying on track. There might be moments when you are tempted to give up, but you won't want to let your partner down!

Defining Your Goals

Working through this process will be more fulfilling if you are working *toward* something. For instance, if your mother has been judgmental about your weight and you're doing this so you can tell her that you've done something about your body, it's unlikely that you'll stick with it through the 40 days. However, if you're doing it so that the next time you see your mother you can feel good about how you look regardless of what she says, then you have an investment to keep going even if you have a difficult day.

Think about what your goals are for yourself. How will you measure success when this process is complete? Perhaps it's being able to enjoy a day of clothing shopping; perhaps it's being able to eat a meal with friends without feeling self-conscious; perhaps it's being able to walk down the street feeling good enough about yourself that you attract some appreciative whistles! Whatever it is, write it in the space below so that you can refer back to it to keep yourself motivated. And *please, PLEASE, PLEASE: **Don't make this a weight-related goal!!! This process is about feeling better in your own skin regardless of your weight!***

_____

_____

_____

_____

_____

_____

with LEAH CAREY

The
Writing
Prompts

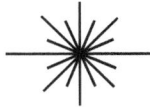

Day #1 – *As a child, what did you hear your mother figure say about her own weight and appearance?*

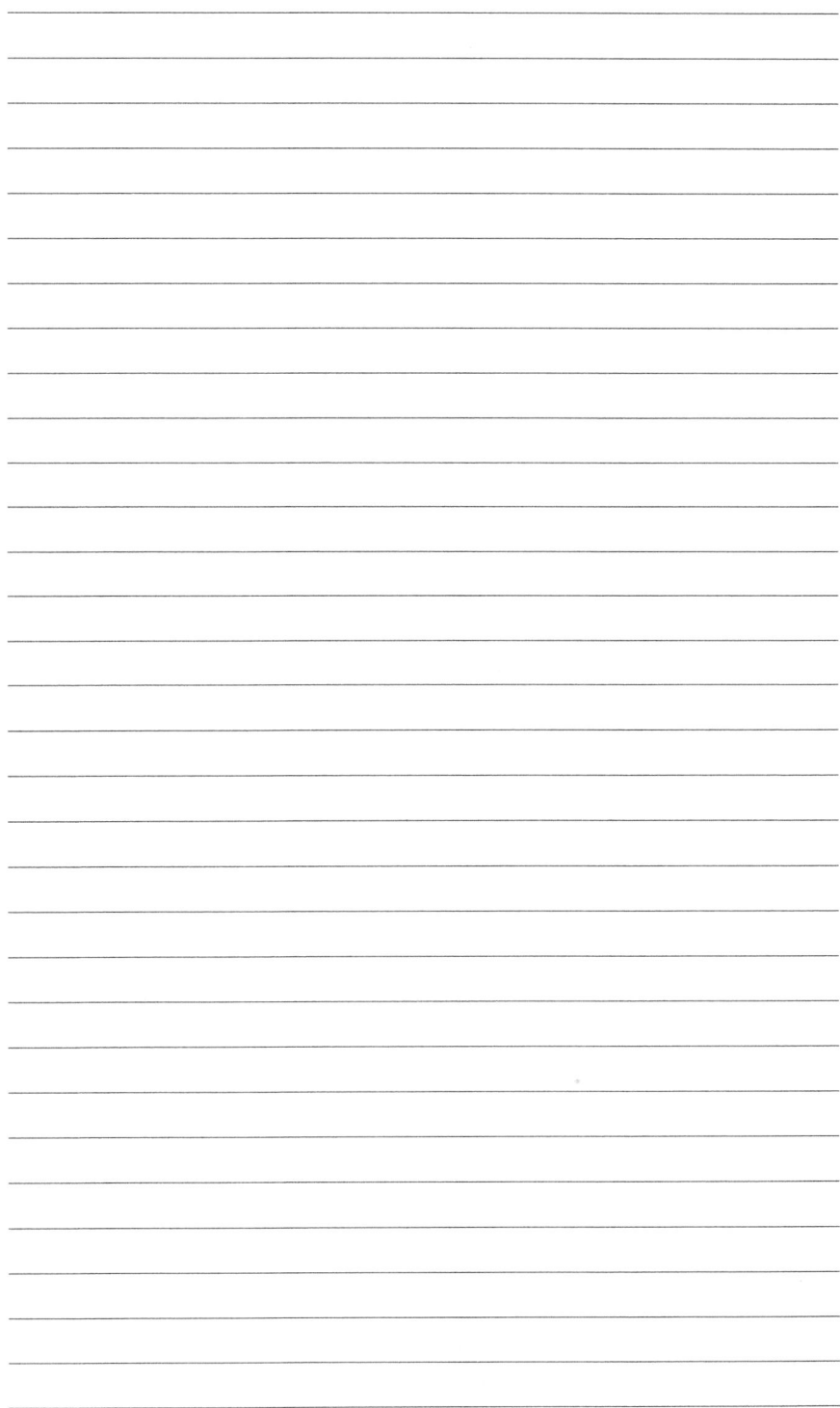

_____

_____

_____

_____

_____

_____

_____

_____

_____

_____

_____

_____

_____

_____

_____

_____

_____

_____

_____

_____

_____

_____

_____

_____

_____

_____

_____

_____

_____

_____

_____

_____

ॐ

Thought for Day #1
It is loving to nurture and be kind to myself.

Day #2 – *As a child, what did you hear your father figure say about his own weight and appearance?*

❧

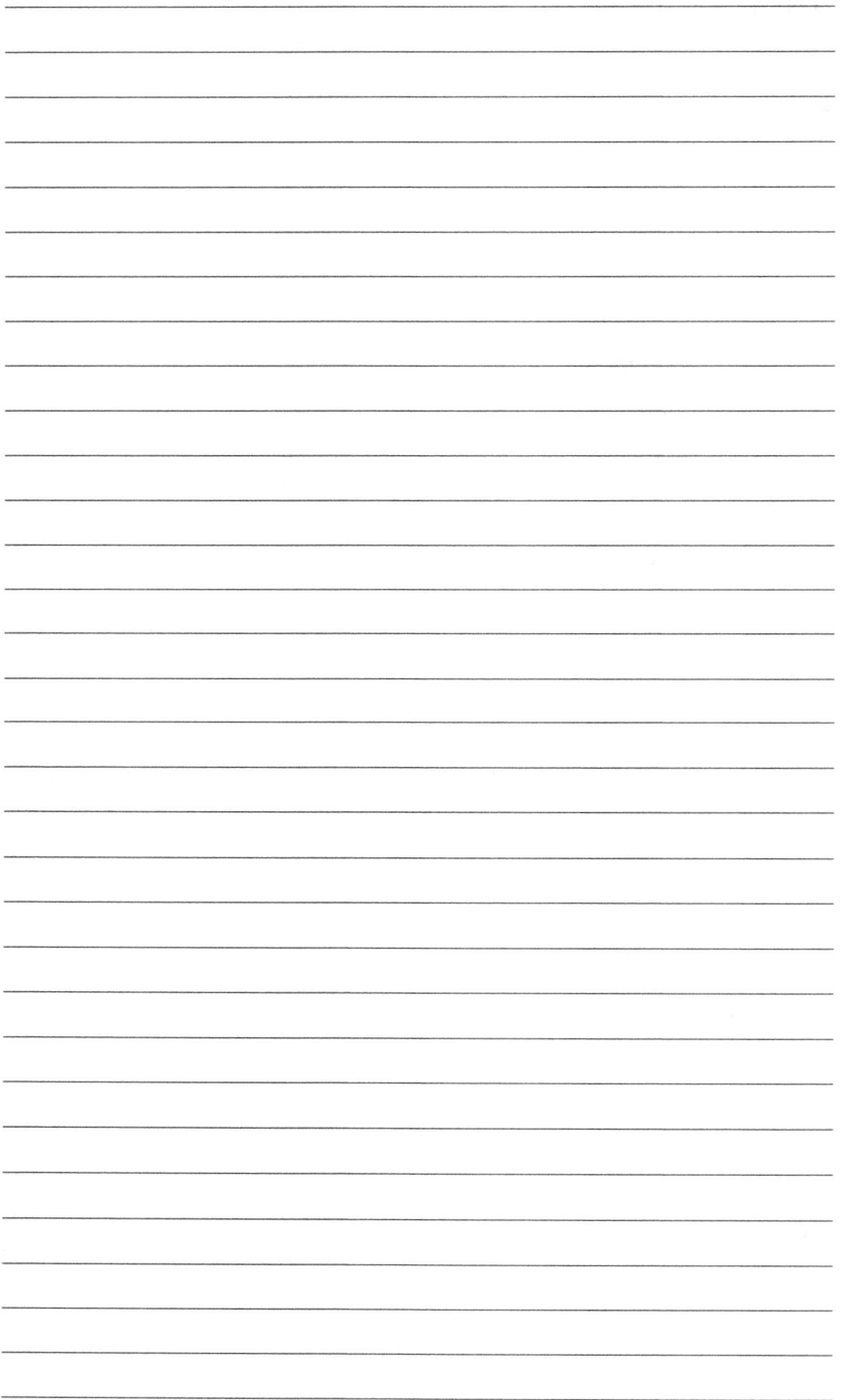

‿✑

Thought for Day #2
God created me just as I am.

Day #3 – *As a child, what did you hear your mother figure say about your weight and appearance?*

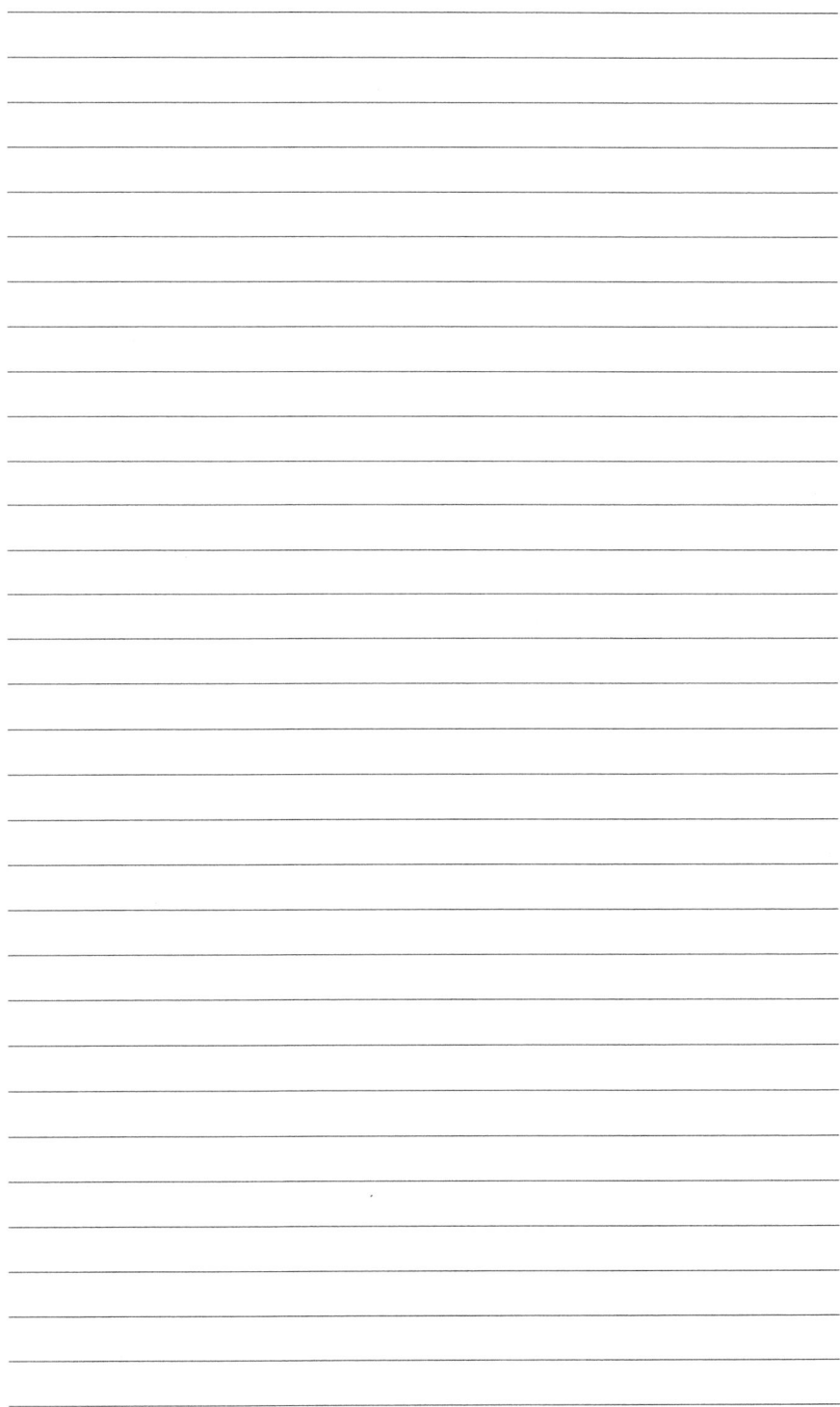

Thought for Day #3

*My life is my own, and I do not need to rely on another person to
tell me who I am.*

Day #4 – *As a child, what did you hear your father figure say about your weight and appearance?*

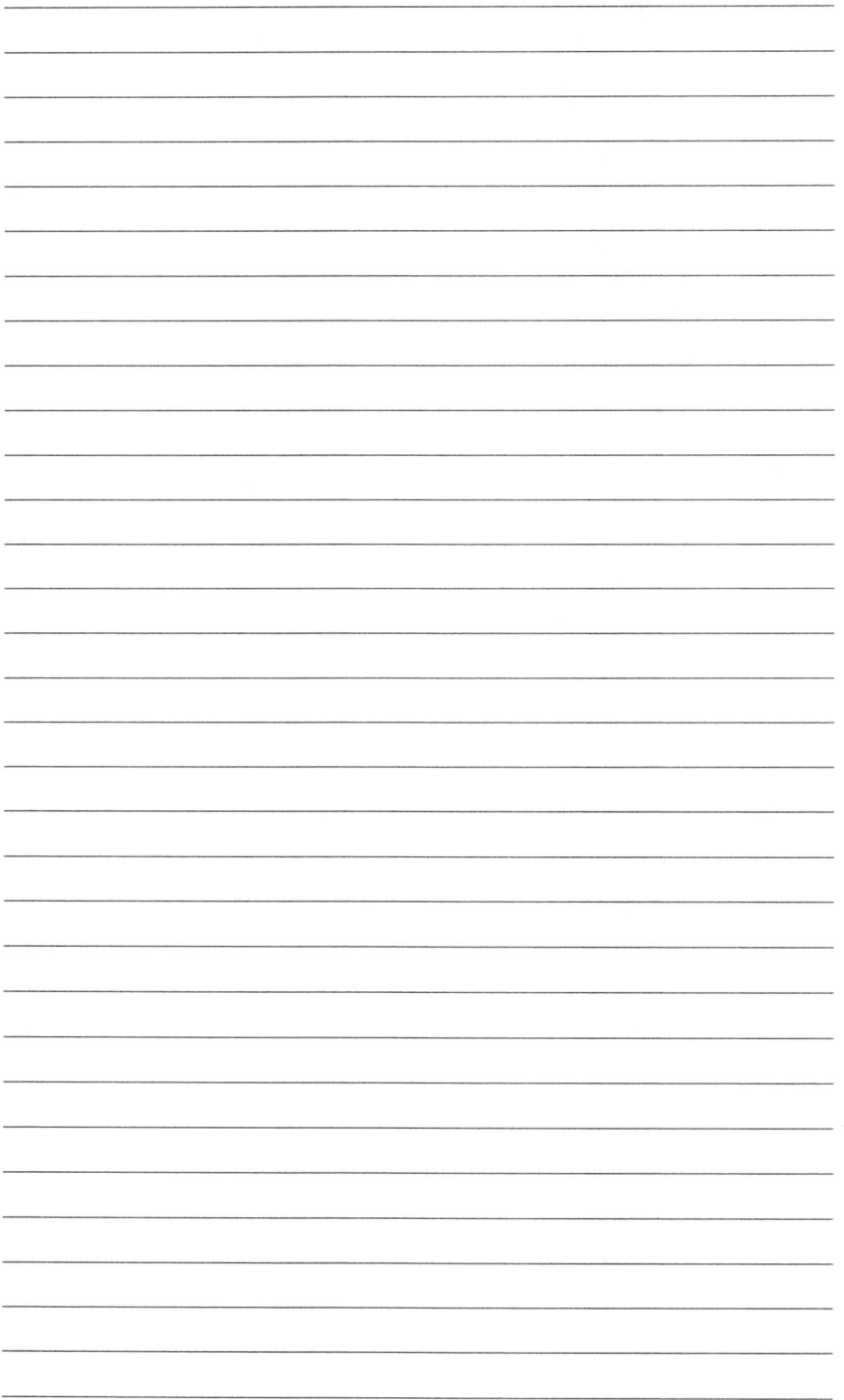

_____

_____

_____

_____

_____

_____

_____

_____

_____

_____

_____

_____

_____

_____

_____

_____

_____

_____

_____

_____

_____

_____

_____

_____

_____

_____

_____

_____

_____

_____

_____

_____

ॐ

Thought for Day #4

My life is my own, and I do not need to rely on another person to tell me how to think and feel about myself.

Day #5 – *Remember a time in your life before you were aware of your weight as an issue. How did you use your body when you were young?*

‍

_____

_____

_____

_____

_____

_____

_____

_____

_____

_____

_____

_____

_____

_____

_____

_____

_____

_____

_____

_____

_____

_____

_____

_____

_____

_____

_____

_____

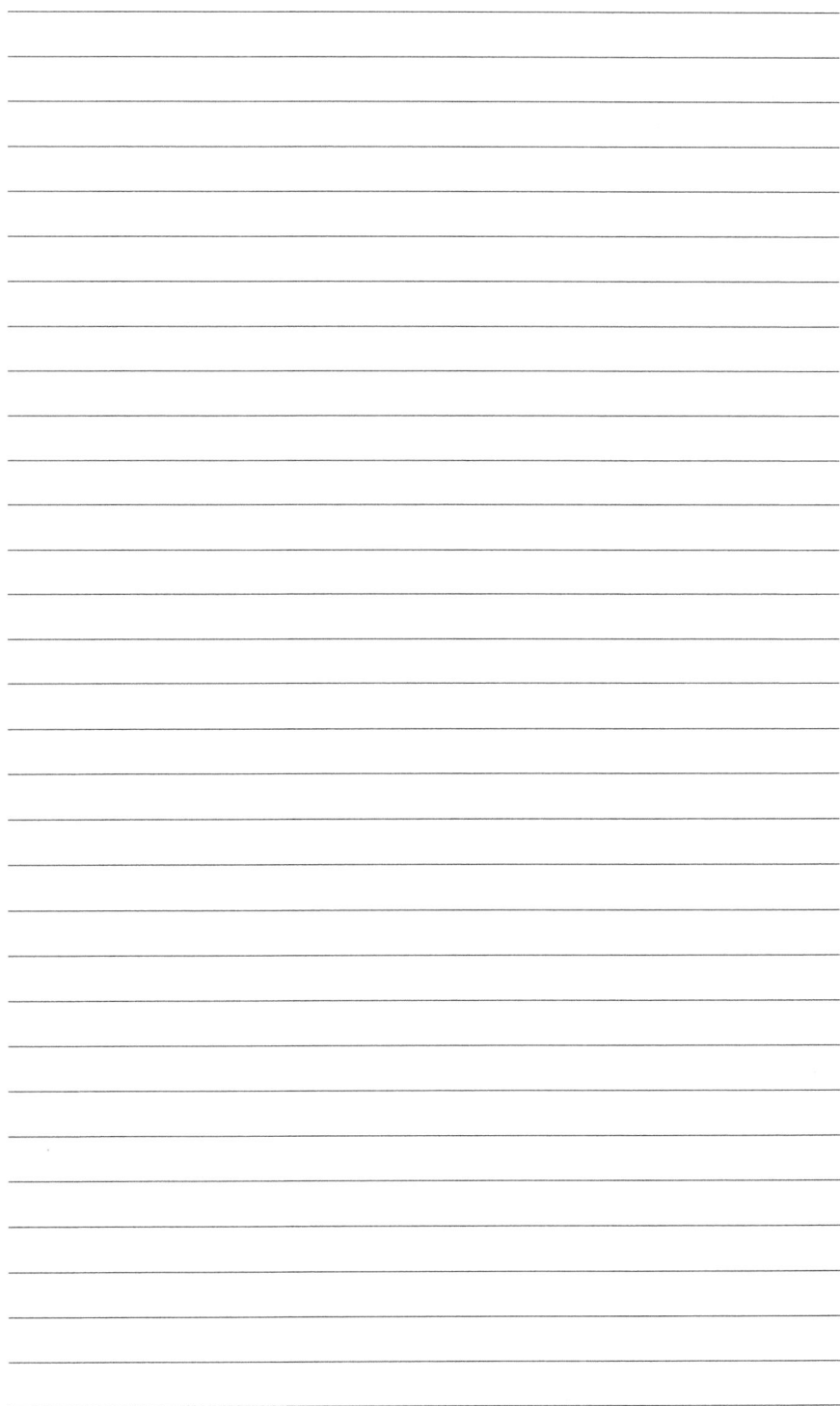

_____

_____

_____

_____

_____

_____

_____

_____

_____

_____

_____

_____

_____

_____

_____

_____

_____

_____

_____

_____

_____

_____

_____

_____

_____

_____

_____

_____

_____

_____

_____

Thought for Day #5
A newborn baby's essential nature is innocence.
All that has changed between my birth and today are my
expectations and beliefs. Today I will remember that
my essential nature is still innocence.

Day #6 – *Describe the first time you became aware of your weight as an issue.*

✍

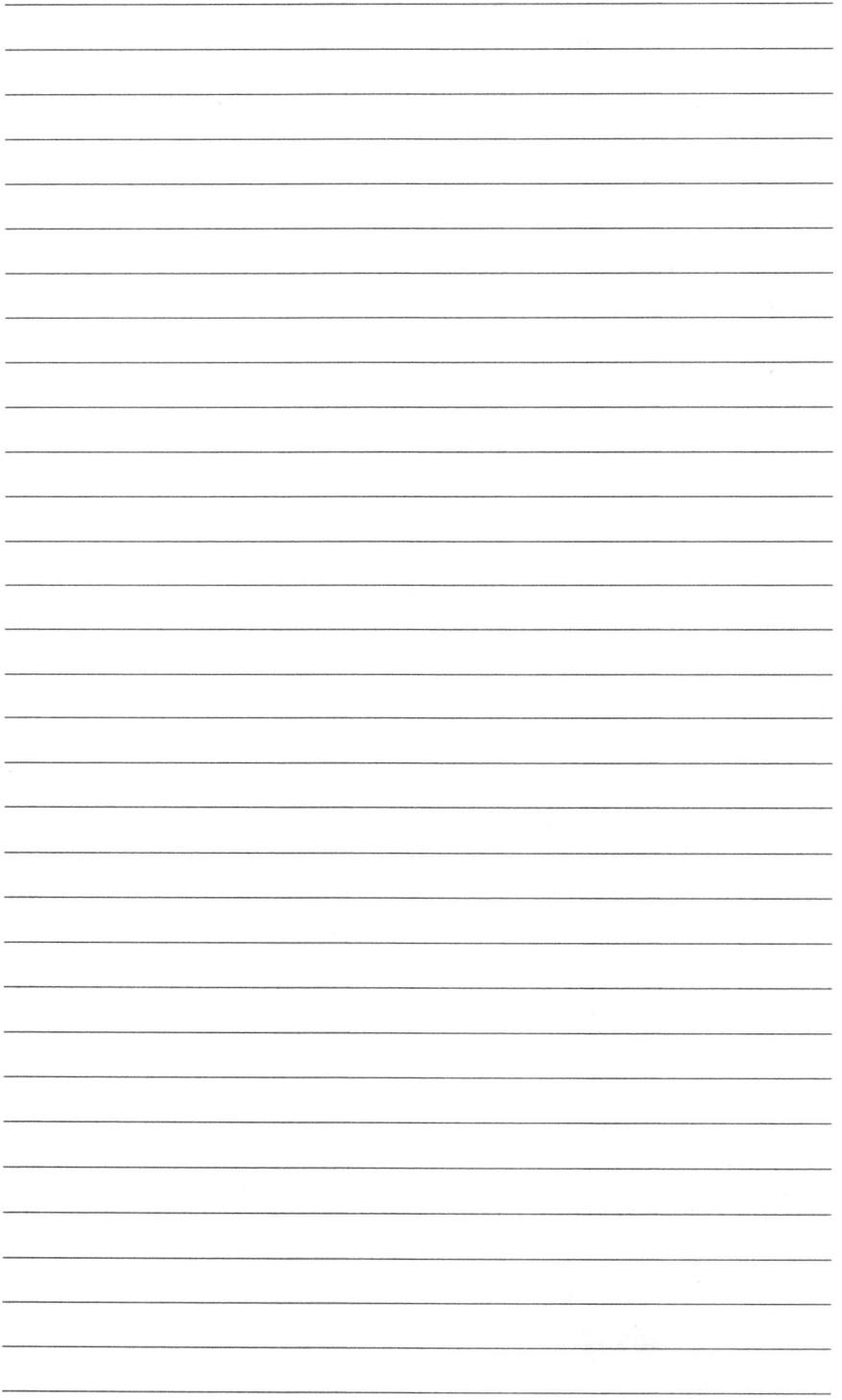

‿ͻ

Thought for Day #6
*Today I will look at myself with childlike innocence and will appreciate
my body for what it does, rather than how it looks.*

Day #7 – *When you look at yourself in the mirror,*
what do you see?

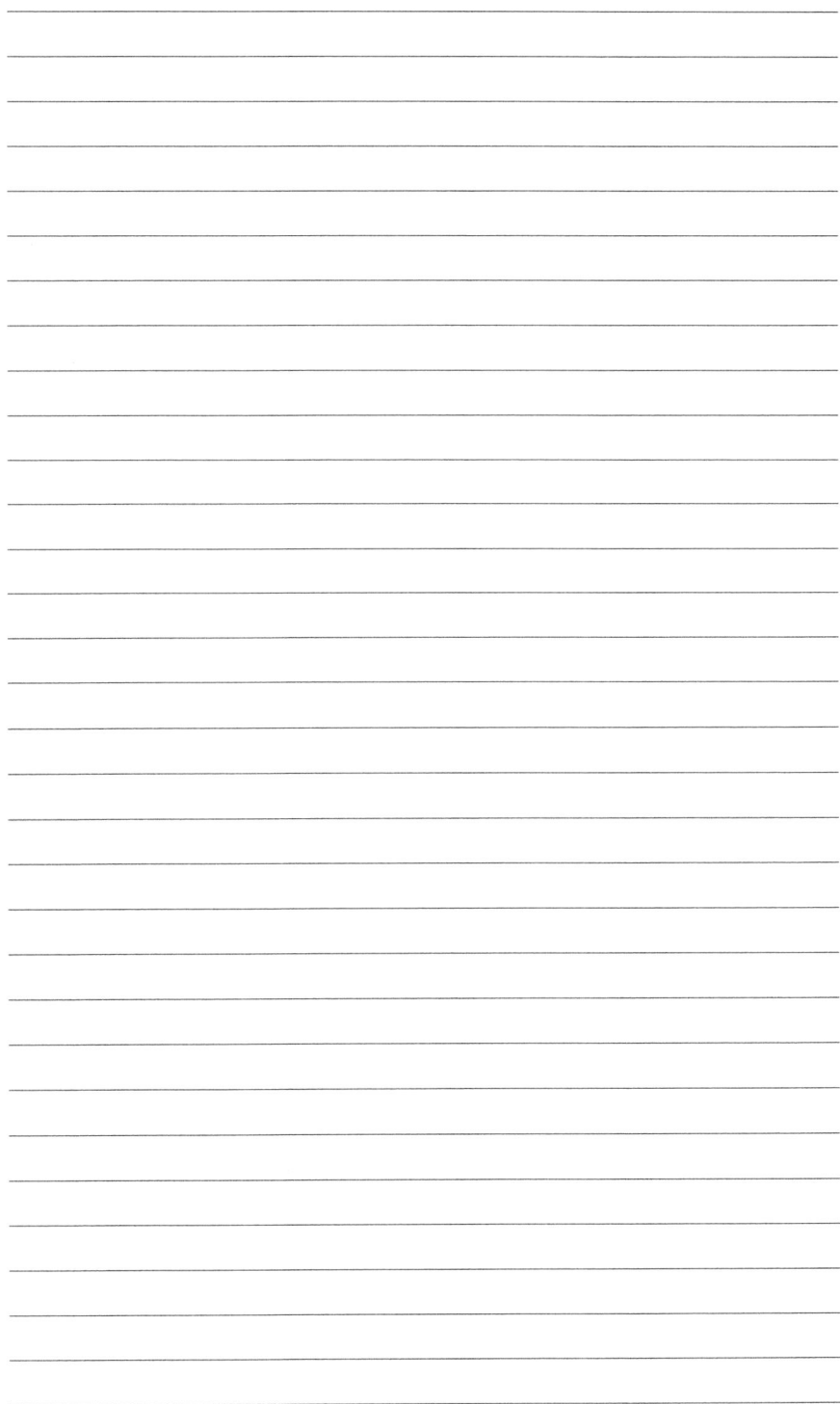

‌

‌

Thought for Day #7
I get to choose what I focus on. Today I will focus on the part(s) of myself that I appreciate.

Day #8 – *Draw a picture of what you see when you look in the mirror (this isn't an art piece – rough shapes are fine). Is this a realistic portrait of what you look like, or have you distorted your body shape in your mind?*

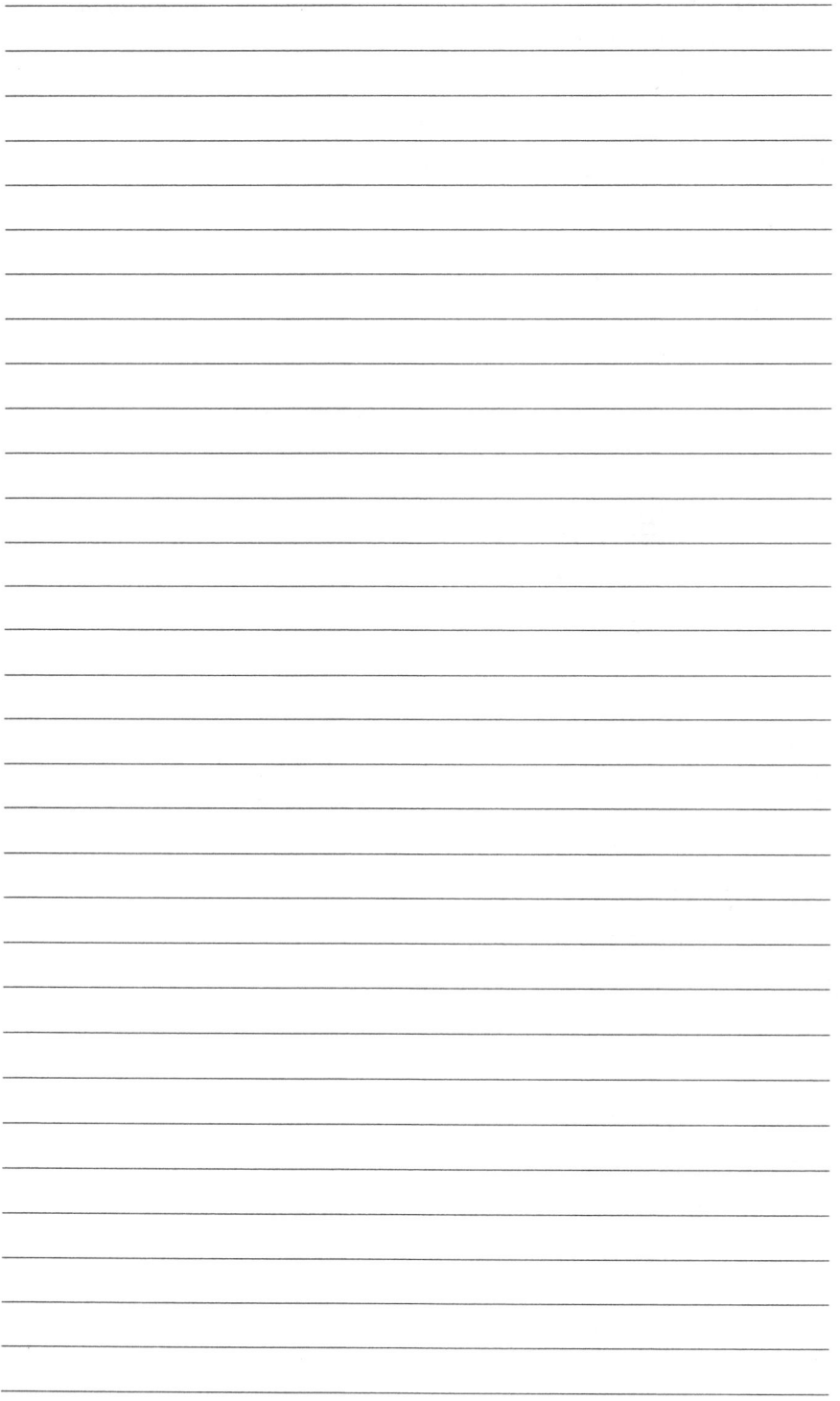

_____

_____

_____

_____

_____

_____

_____

_____

_____

_____

_____

_____

_____

_____

_____

_____

_____

_____

_____

_____

_____

_____

_____

_____

_____

_____

_____

_____

_____

℘

Thought for Day #8
The way that I see my body in the mirror is probably not accurate. Today I choose to see myself as I truly am.

Day #9 – *When you look at yourself in the mirror, what do you <u>wish</u> you were seeing?*

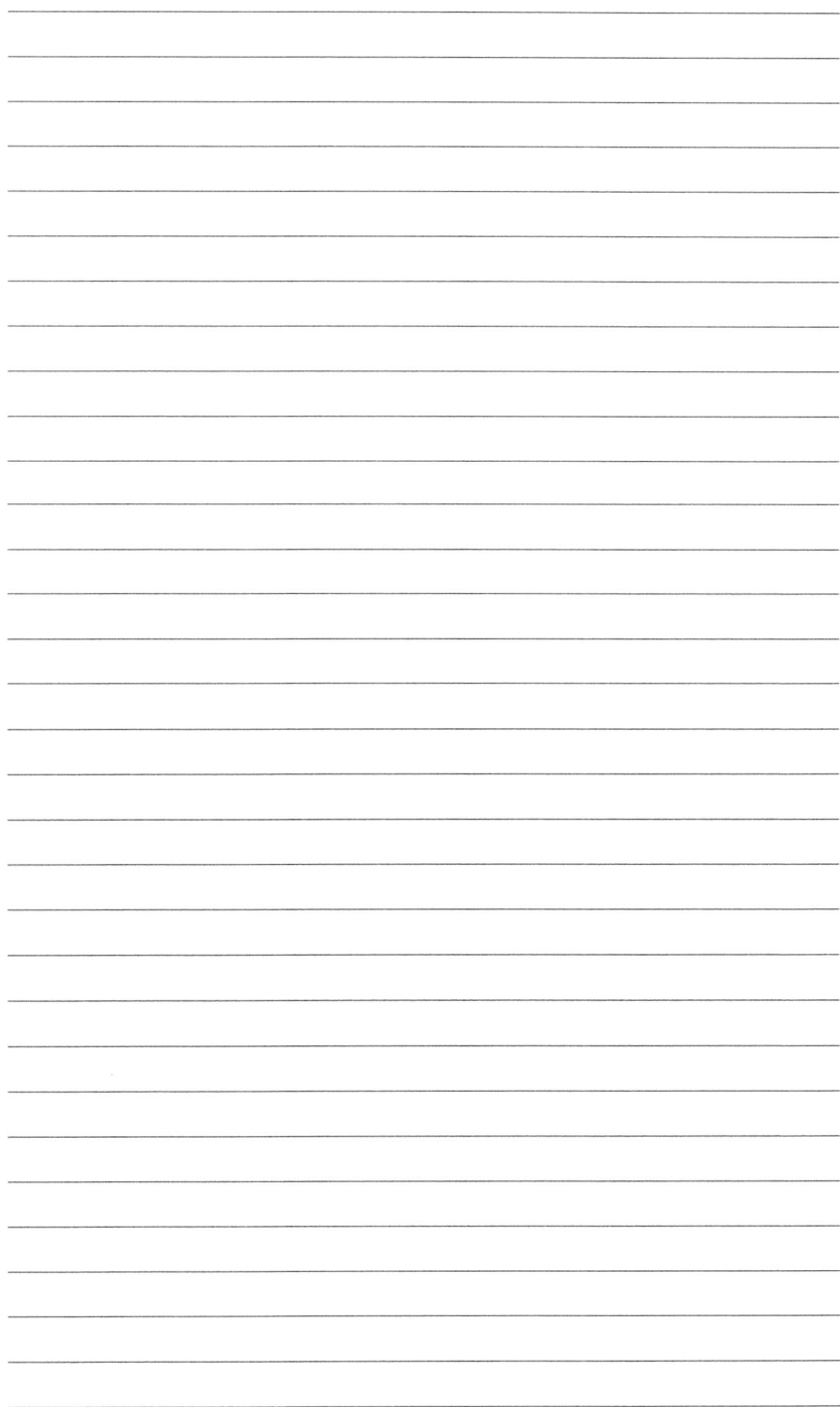

_____

_____

_____

_____

_____

_____

_____

_____

_____

_____

_____

_____

_____

_____

_____

_____

_____

_____

_____

_____

_____

_____

_____

_____

_____

_____

_____

_____

_____

_____

_____

_____

_____

_____

_____

_____

ം

_____

Thought for Day #9

*There is a difference between wishful thinking (which makes me feel
worse about myself) and creative thinking (which finds new solutions
to old problems). Today I will focus on thinking creatively.*

Day #10 – *Draw a picture of what you wish you saw in the mirror (rough shapes). Is this image a realistic possibility or an idealized fantasy?*

ᴽ

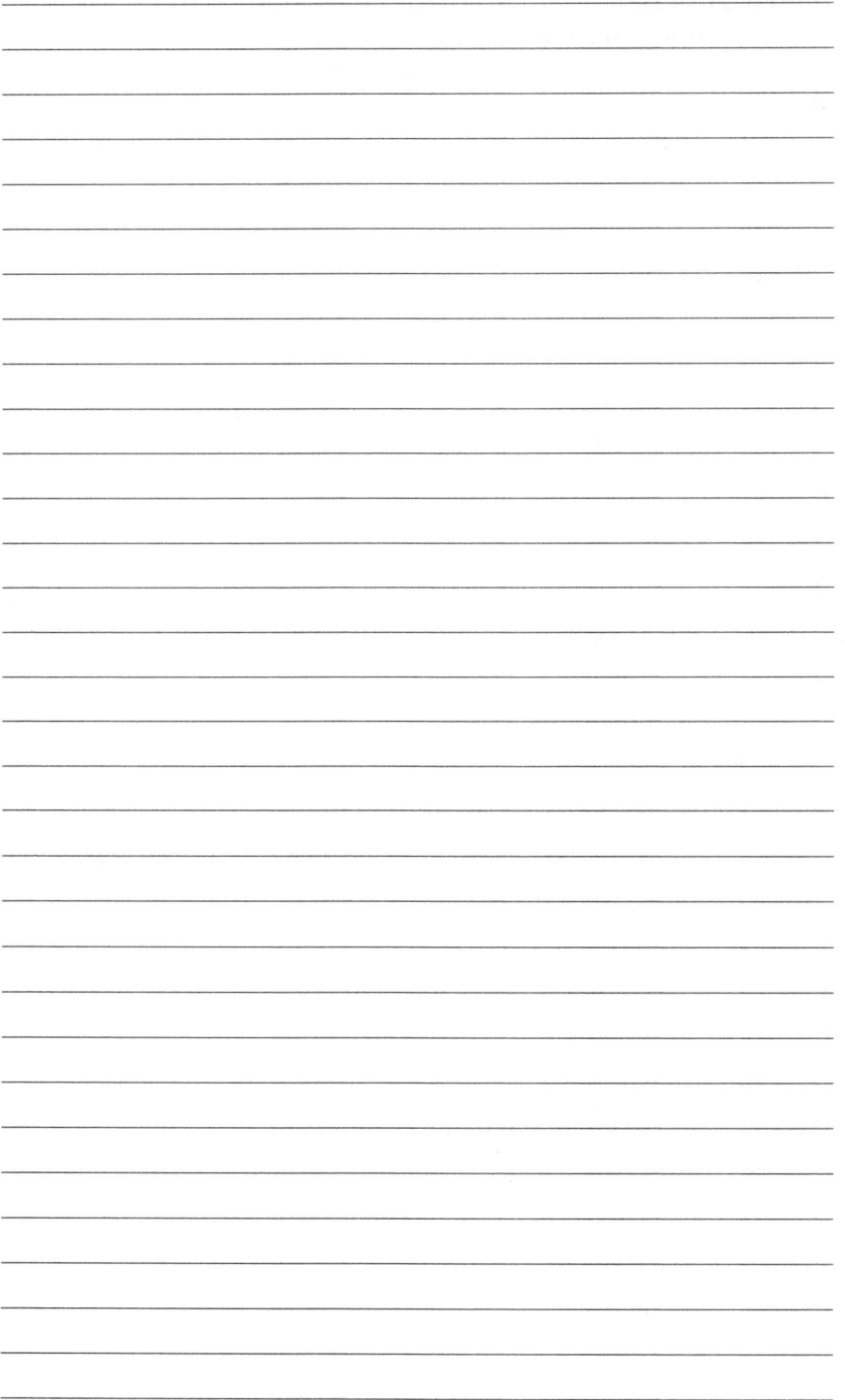

_____

_____

_____

_____

_____

_____

_____

_____

_____

_____

_____

_____

_____

_____

_____

_____

_____

_____

_____

_____

_____

_____

_____

_____

_____

_____

_____

_____

℘

_____

Thought for Day #10

Today I choose to see myself as I truly am. The body I see in the mirror may have flaws, but it gets me where I'm going each day.

Day #11 – *What was your experience of food shopping and meal preparation when you were a child?*

~

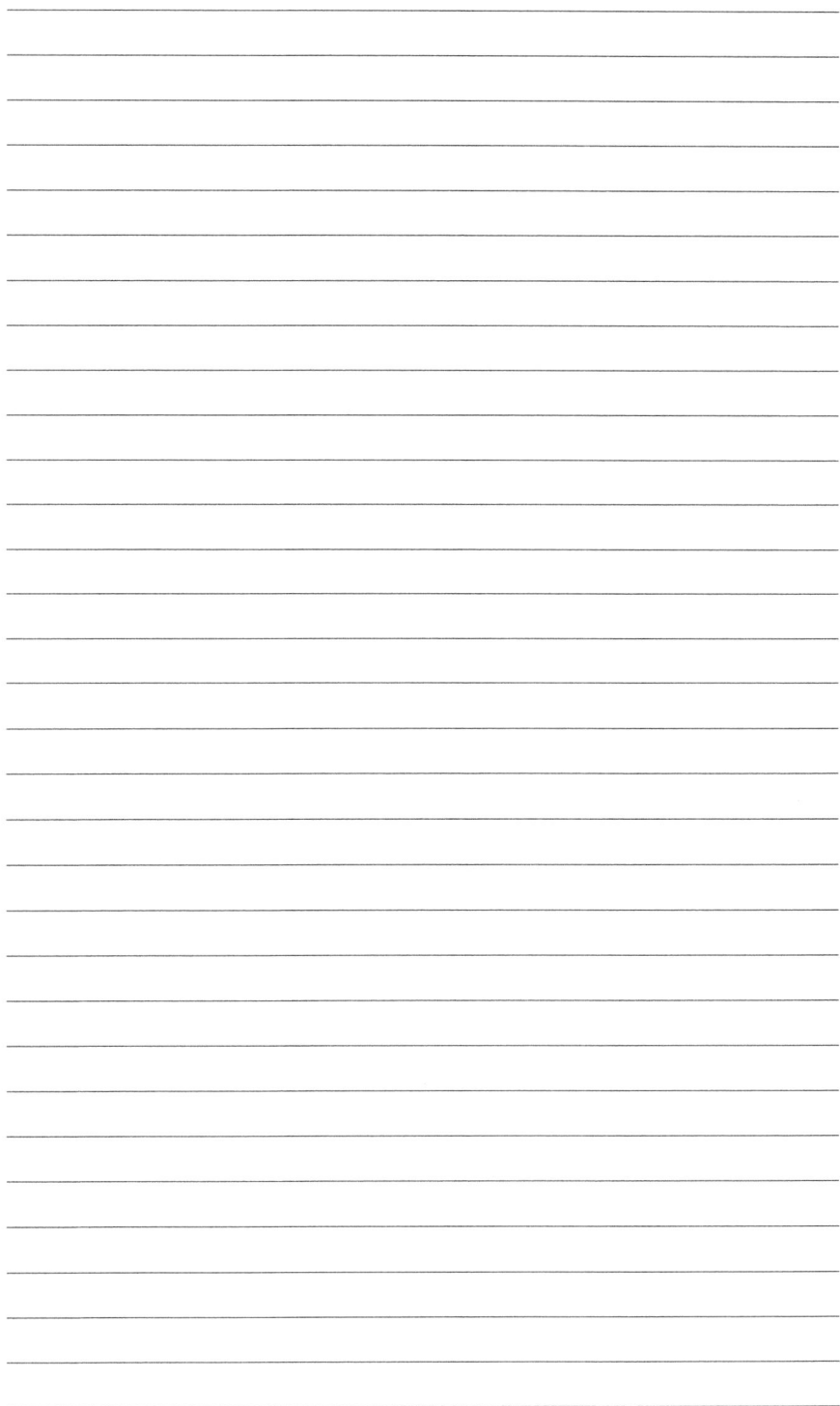

ↄ

Thought for Day #11
Today I am in charge of caring for myself, and I can choose
how to use food, the most basic form of nourishment.

Day #12 – *Identify a part of your body that you dislike. What practical function does that part of your body play in your day-to-day life?*

❧

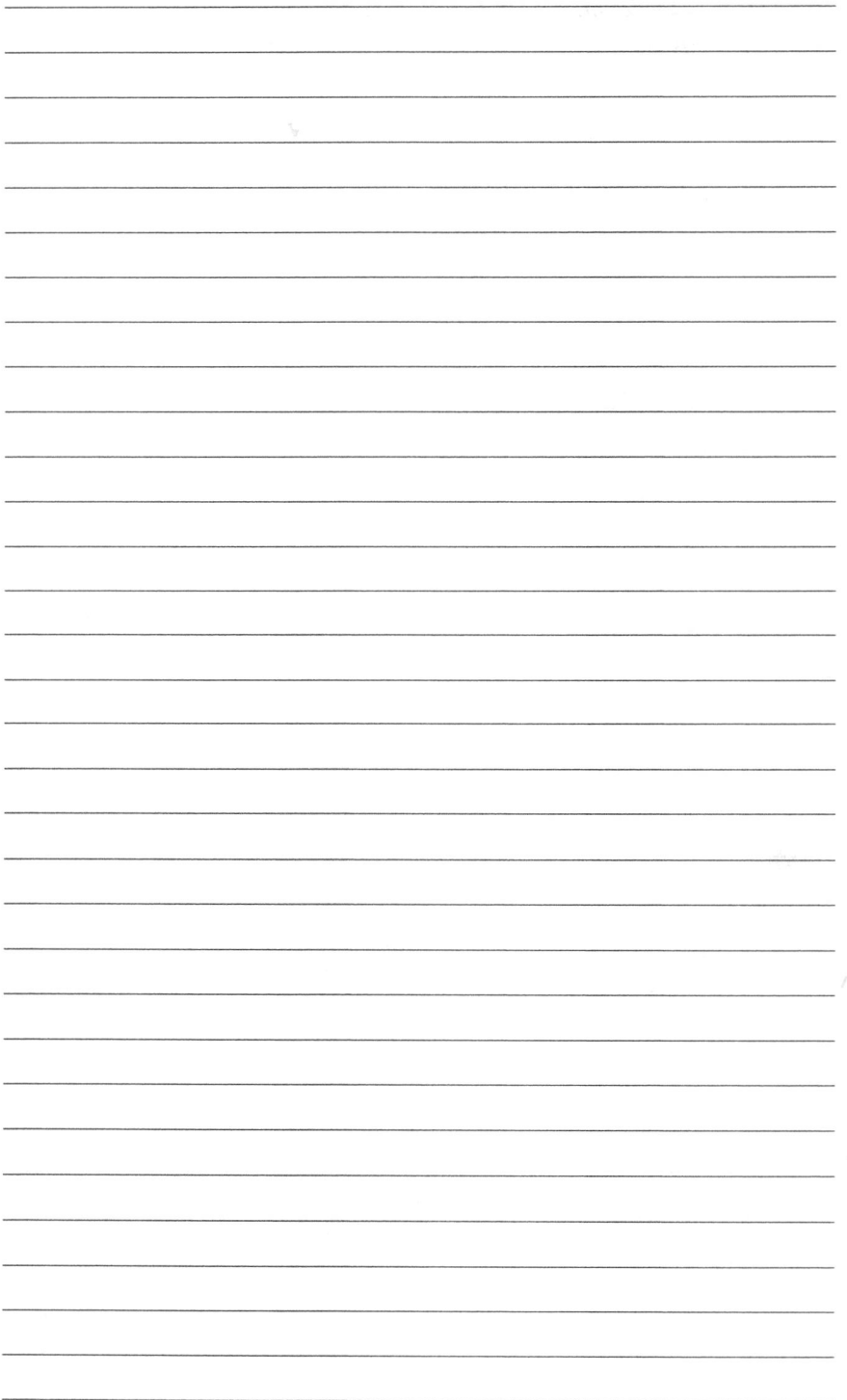

_____

_____

_____

_____

_____

_____

_____

_____

_____

_____

_____

_____

_____

_____

_____

_____

_____

_____

_____

_____

_____

_____

_____

_____

_____

_____

_____

_____

_____

_____

_____

_____

_____

ॐ

Thought for Day #12
*Everything created in nature has a purpose. Today I'll focus on what my
body can accomplish, rather than how I think it looks.*

Day #13 – *Identify a part of your body that you like. What practical function does it play in your day-to-day life?*

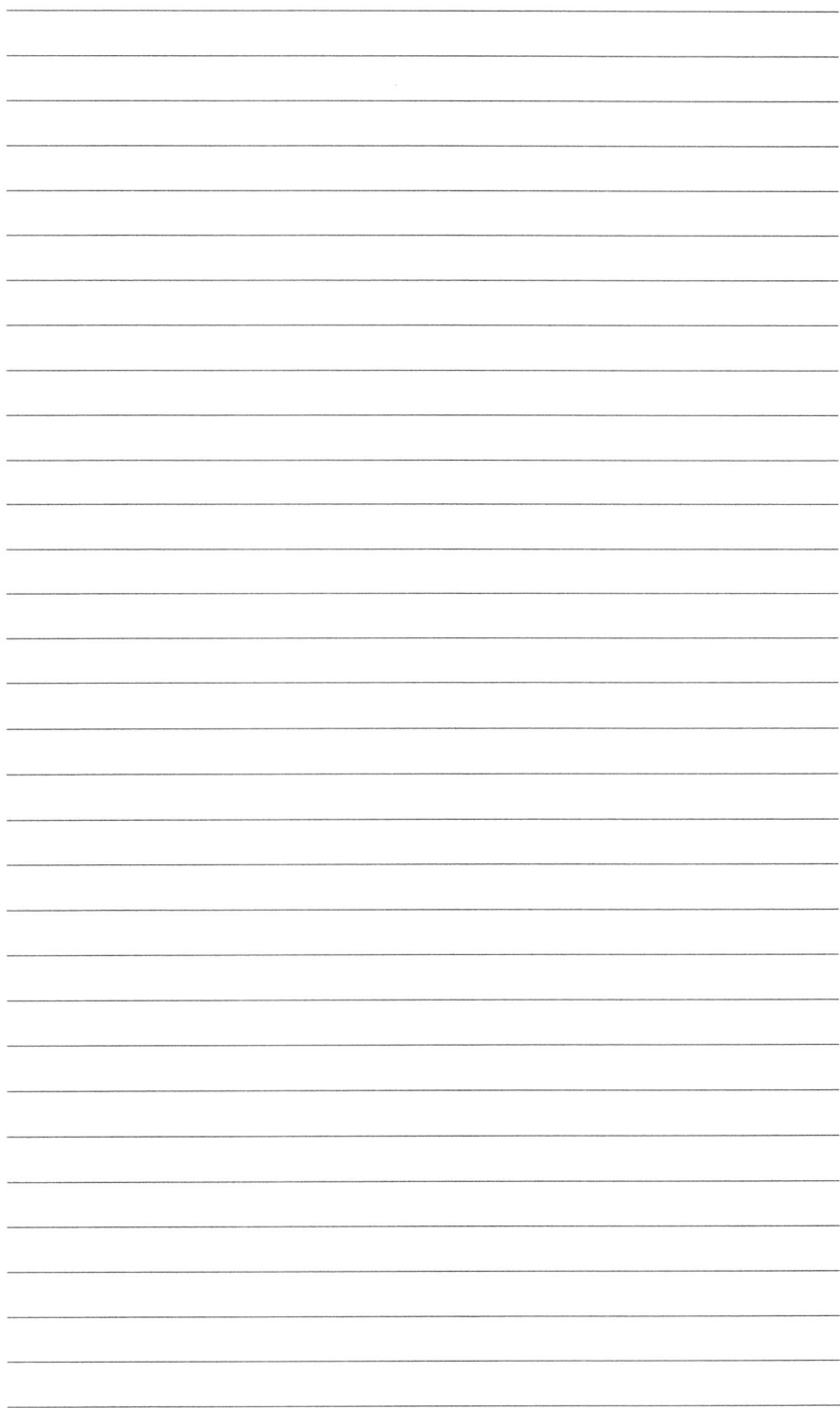

ço

Thought for Day #13

*Everything created in nature has a purpose. Today I will focus
on how my body works, rather than how I think it looks.*

Day #14 – *Describe how you felt about your body during your first sexual experience. How has that feeling changed? How has it remained the same?*

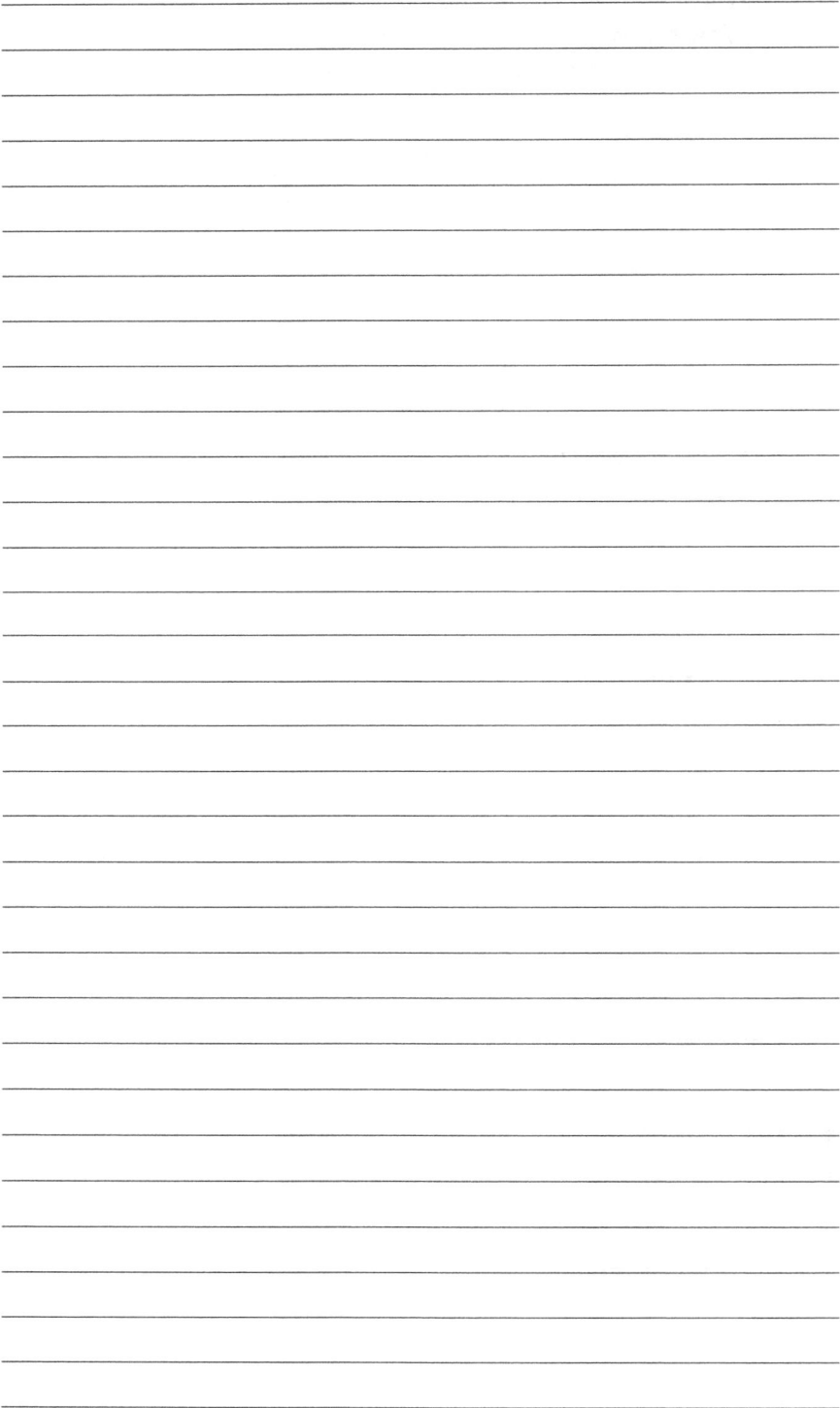

Thought for Day #14
My body is my temple. Today, and every day in the future,
I invite only people who respect my body to touch it.

Day #15 – *Make a list of things that your body does well (and that you do well in your body).*

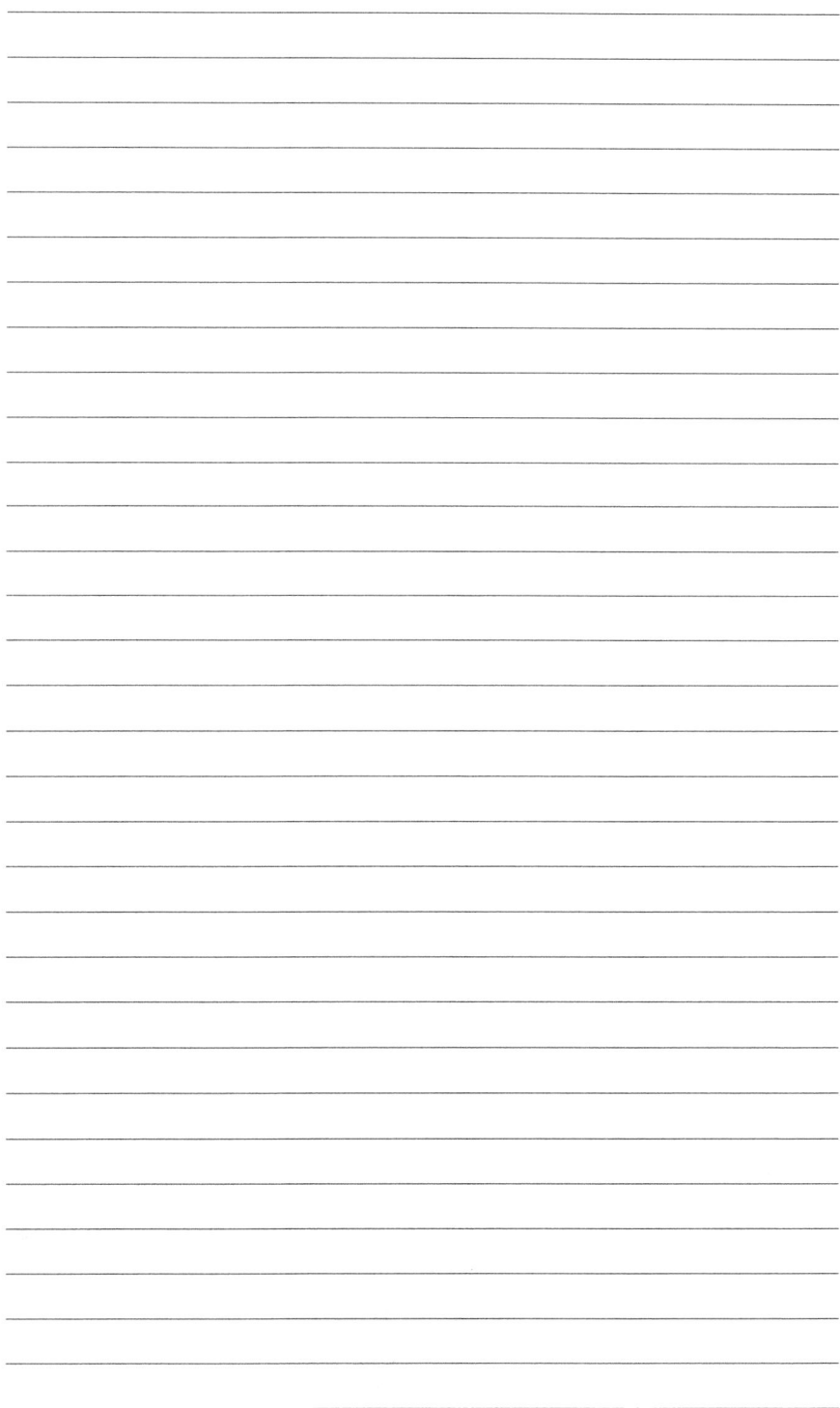

_____

_____

_____

_____

_____

_____

_____

_____

_____

_____

_____

_____

_____

_____

_____

_____

_____

_____

_____

_____

_____

_____

_____

_____

_____

_____

_____

_____

ॐ
_____

Thought for Day #15
My body is my temple.
Today I choose to appreciate this sacred space.

Day #16 – *Describe a time when someone treated you poorly*
because of your appearance.
What would you like to say to that person now?

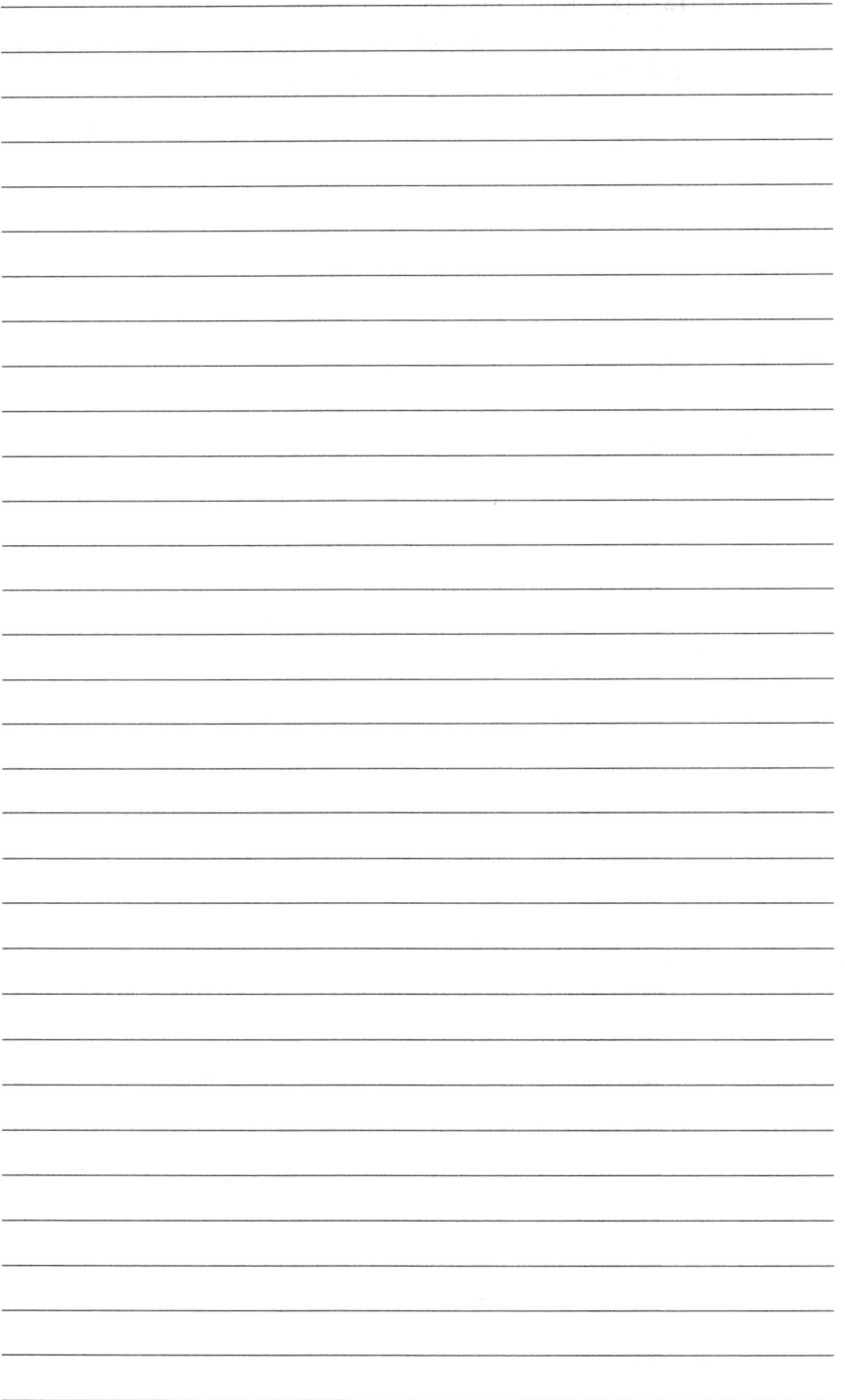

_____

_____

_____

_____

_____

_____

_____

_____

_____

_____

_____

_____

_____

_____

_____

_____

_____

_____

_____

_____

_____

_____

_____

_____

_____

_____

_____

_____

_____

_____

ॐ

Thought for Day #16
*Today I will remember that I get to choose what I believe. If I hear
something hurtful, I don't have to believe it.*

Day #17 – *Describe a time when you treated someone else poorly (verbally or in your mind) because of their appearance. BE HONEST! What would you like to say to that person now?*

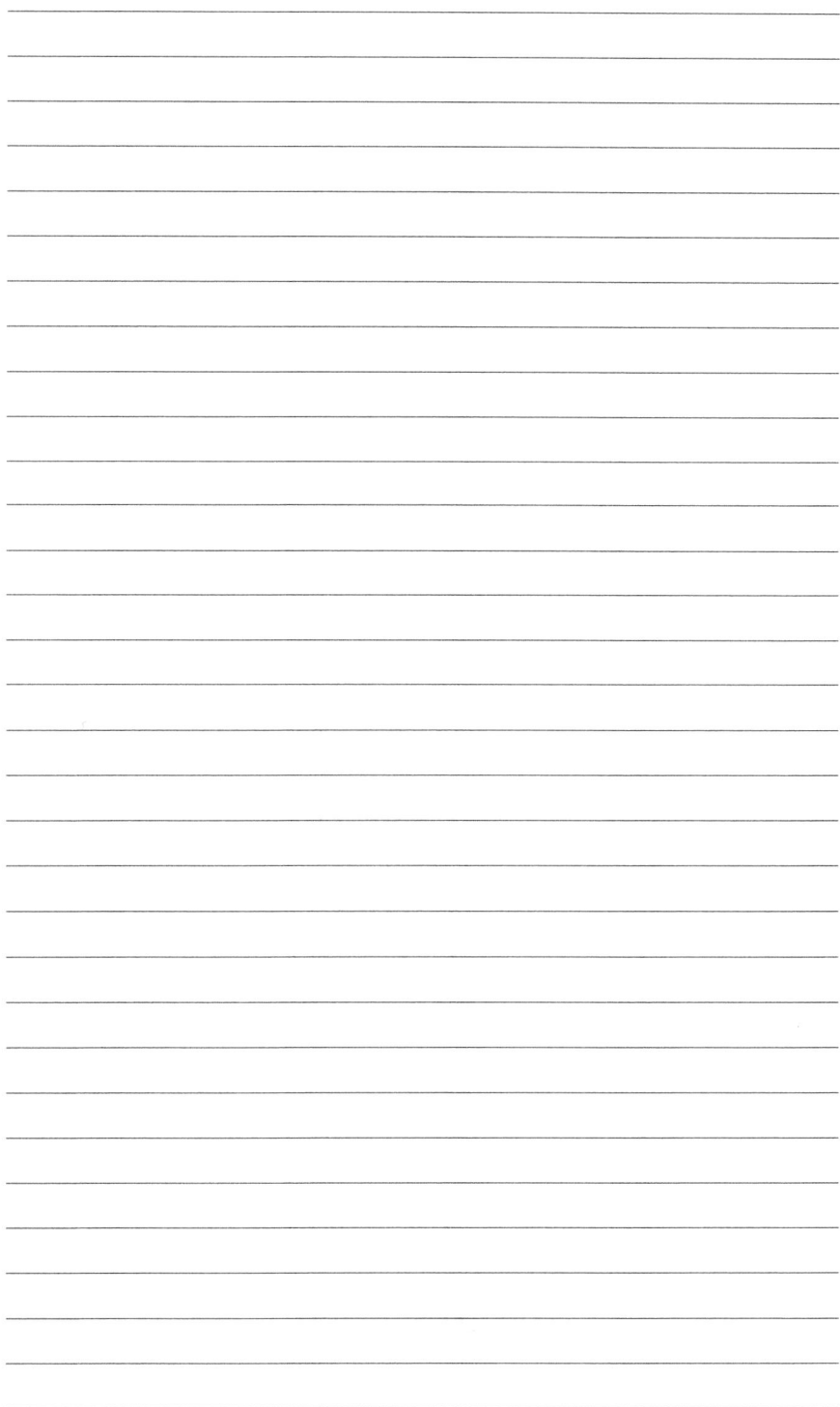

‏ݎ‎

Thought for Day #17
Today, before I speak to anyone, I will ask myself three things:
Is what I have to say kind? Is it true? Is it necessary?

Day #18 – *Describe a time when you attempted to lose weight but didn't (or lost weight and then gained it back). Why do you believe that happened? In answering this, look at your own thoughts and motivations rather than at outside circumstances.*

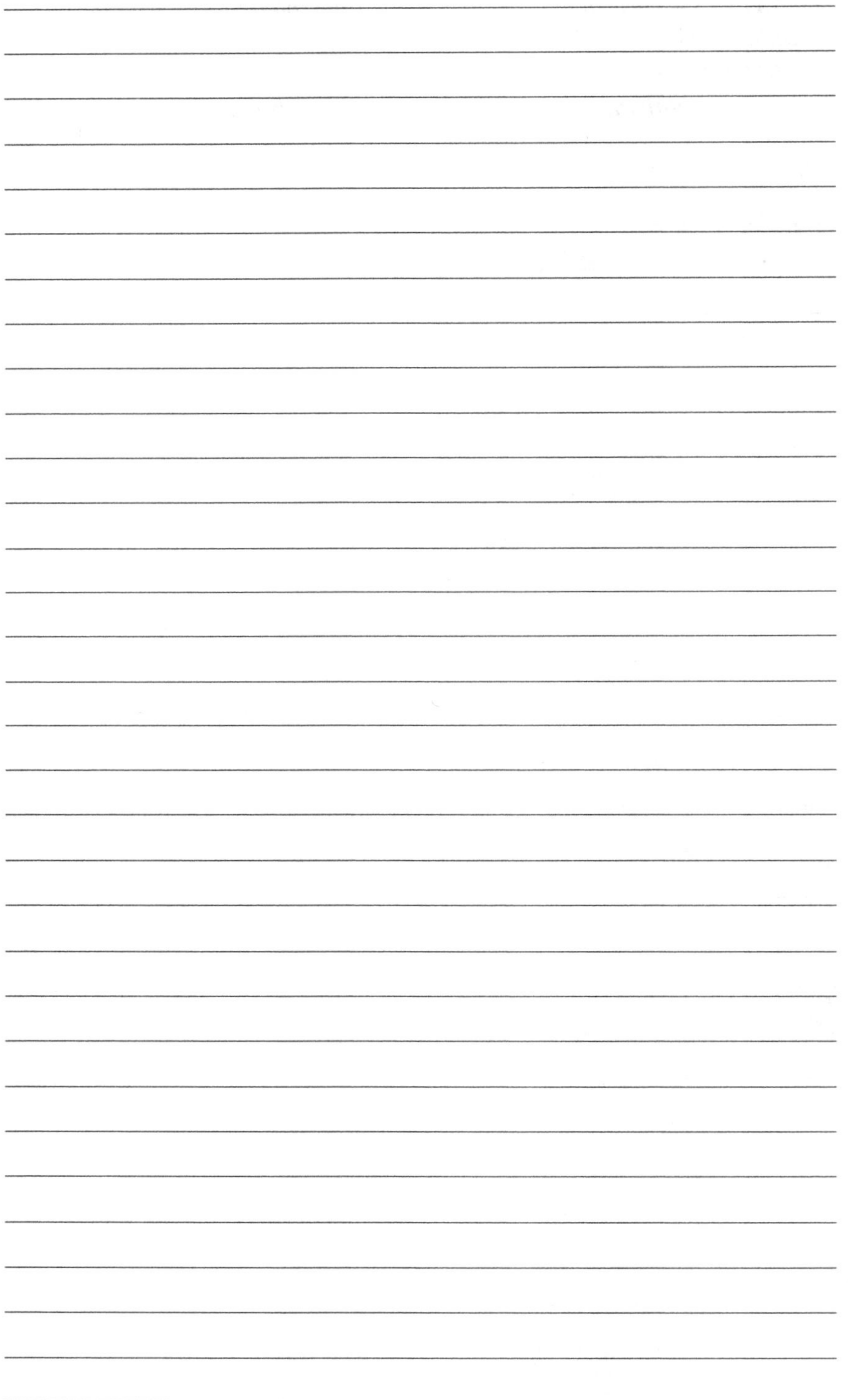

Thought for Day #18

Nobody is perfect. Today I will accept myself for who I am at this moment.

Day #19 – *Describe your experience of watching television, reading magazines, or engaging with other popular media. How do you feel about yourself when you do these things?*

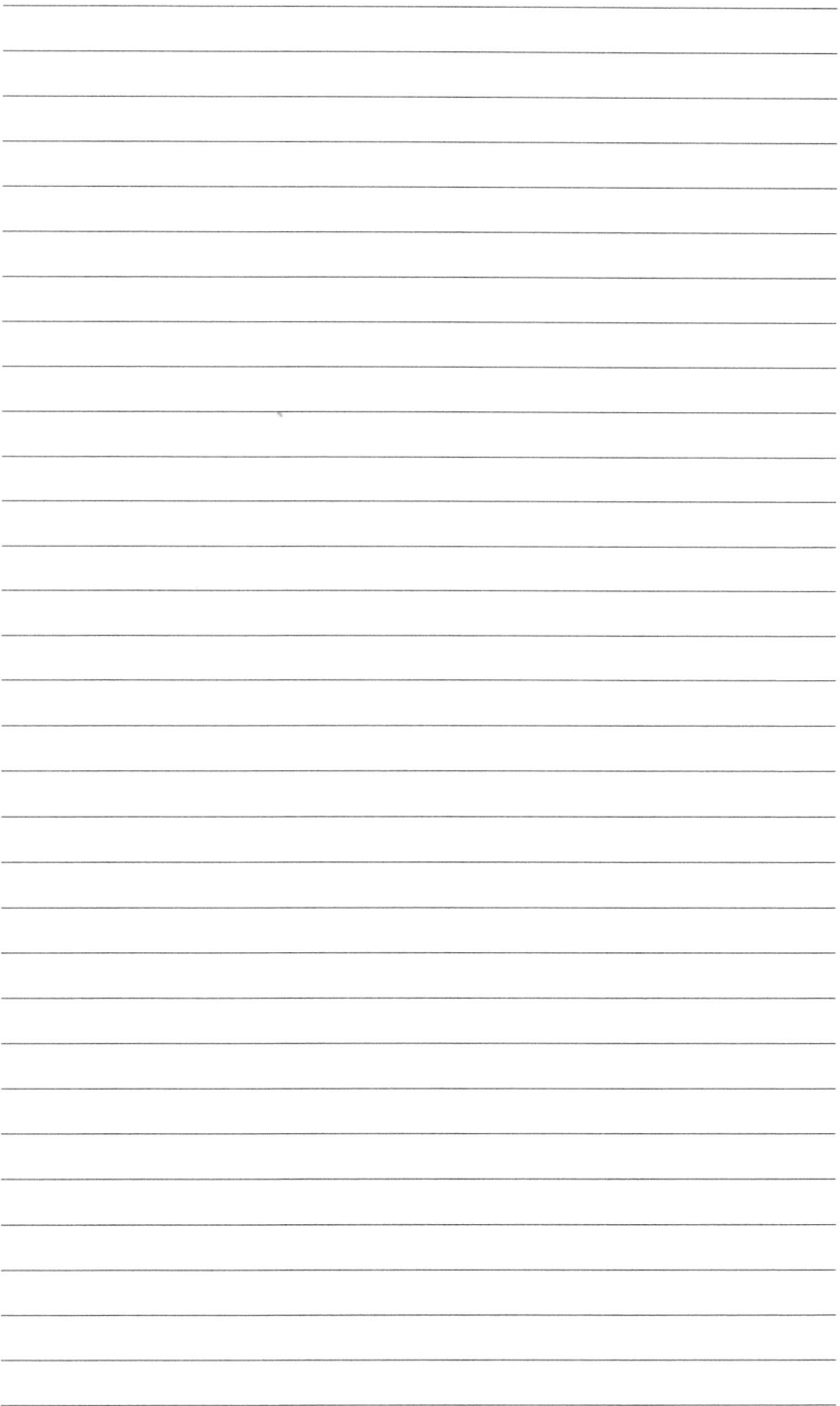

_____

ॐ

Thought for Day #19
*Today, practice a media blackout. Don't look at magazines, TV,
or celebrity news. At the end of the day, notice how you feel.*

Day #20 – *What is one SMALL thing you can do each day to feel better about yourself? Let this be concrete – something you wear, something you read, something you do, etc. Describe how you think this one small action will help you feel better about yourself.*

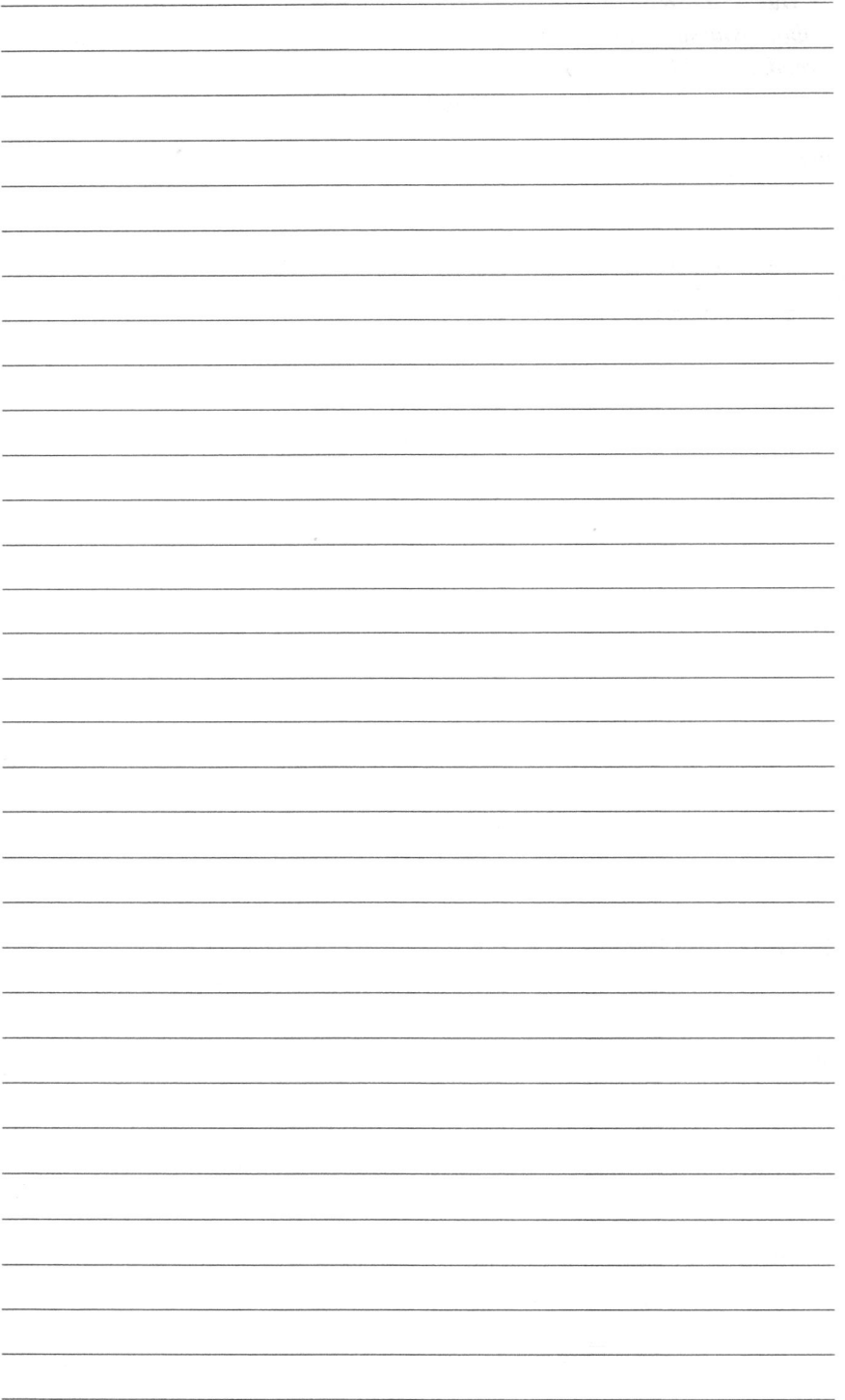

_____

_____

_____

_____

_____

_____

_____

_____

_____

_____

_____

_____

_____

_____

_____

_____

_____

_____

_____

_____

_____

_____

_____

_____

_____

_____

_____

_____

_____

_____

_____

_____

_____ ∽

_____

Thought for Day #20
I can choose how I feel.
When I do good things for myself, I feel good!

Day #21 – *Describe a time when you felt really sexy. What were your thoughts about yourself in that moment? What do you believe caused you to feel that way?*

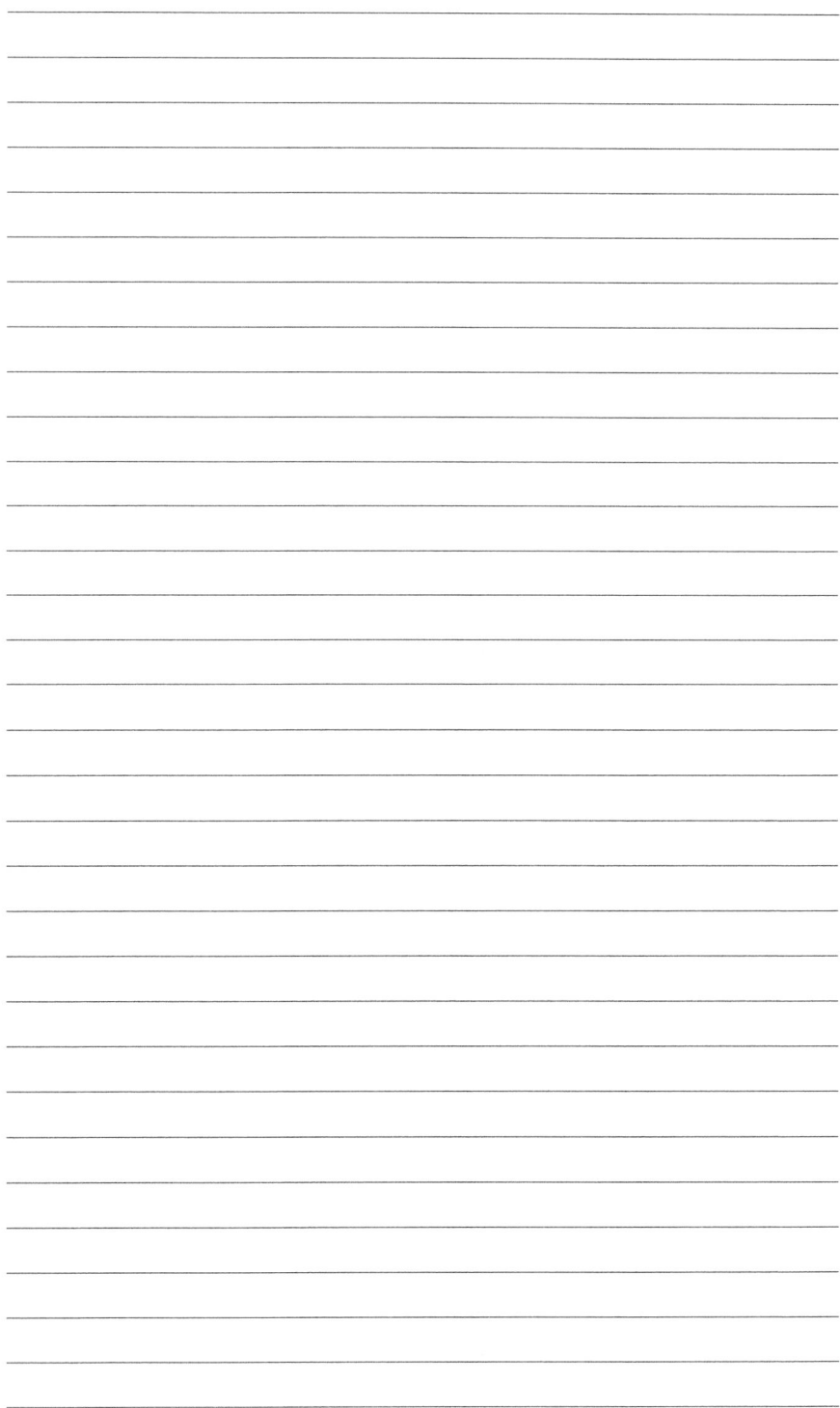

Thought for Day #21

Sexy is a state of mind, not a state of body. Today I will remember what sexy feels like!

Day #22 – *Describe your main stress-coping mechanism (for example – do you eat? watch TV? sleep? start an argument? meditate? exercise?) Does this coping mechanism make you feel better or worse about yourself?*

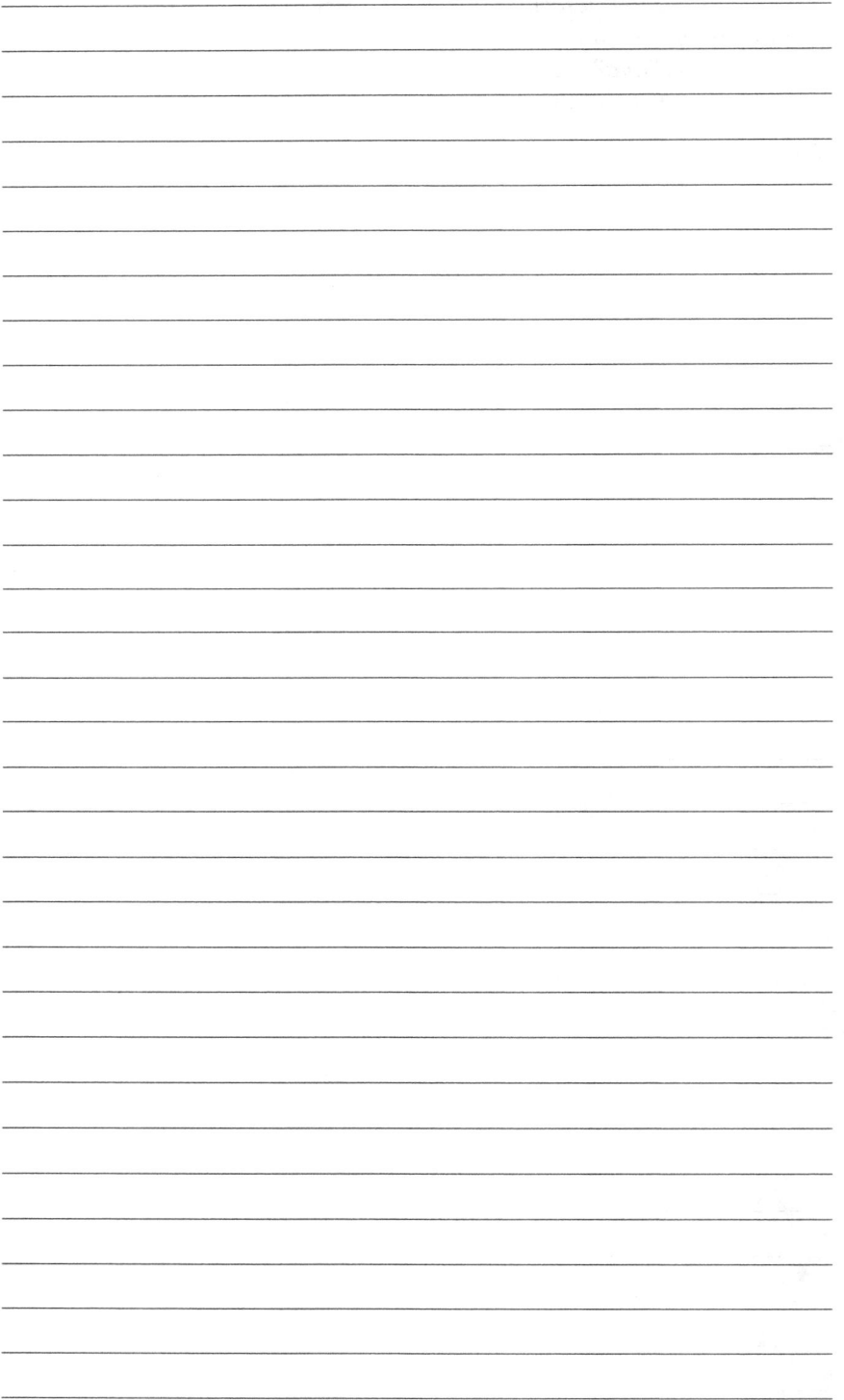

_____

_____

_____

_____

_____

_____

_____

_____

_____

_____

_____

_____

_____

_____

_____

_____

_____

_____

_____

_____

_____

_____

_____

_____

_____

_____

_____

ର

Thought for Day #22
Stress is not always a bad thing… it's how I deal with it
that isn't always healthy. Today I will be aware of my
reaction to stress, and I will remember that
I can make a different choice.

Day #23 – *Imagine that life is exactly the way you want it – job, relationship, home, family, finances, friends, etc. – but your body looks exactly as it is today. Can you be happy in the midst of perfection, even if you don't consider your body to be perfect?*

✐

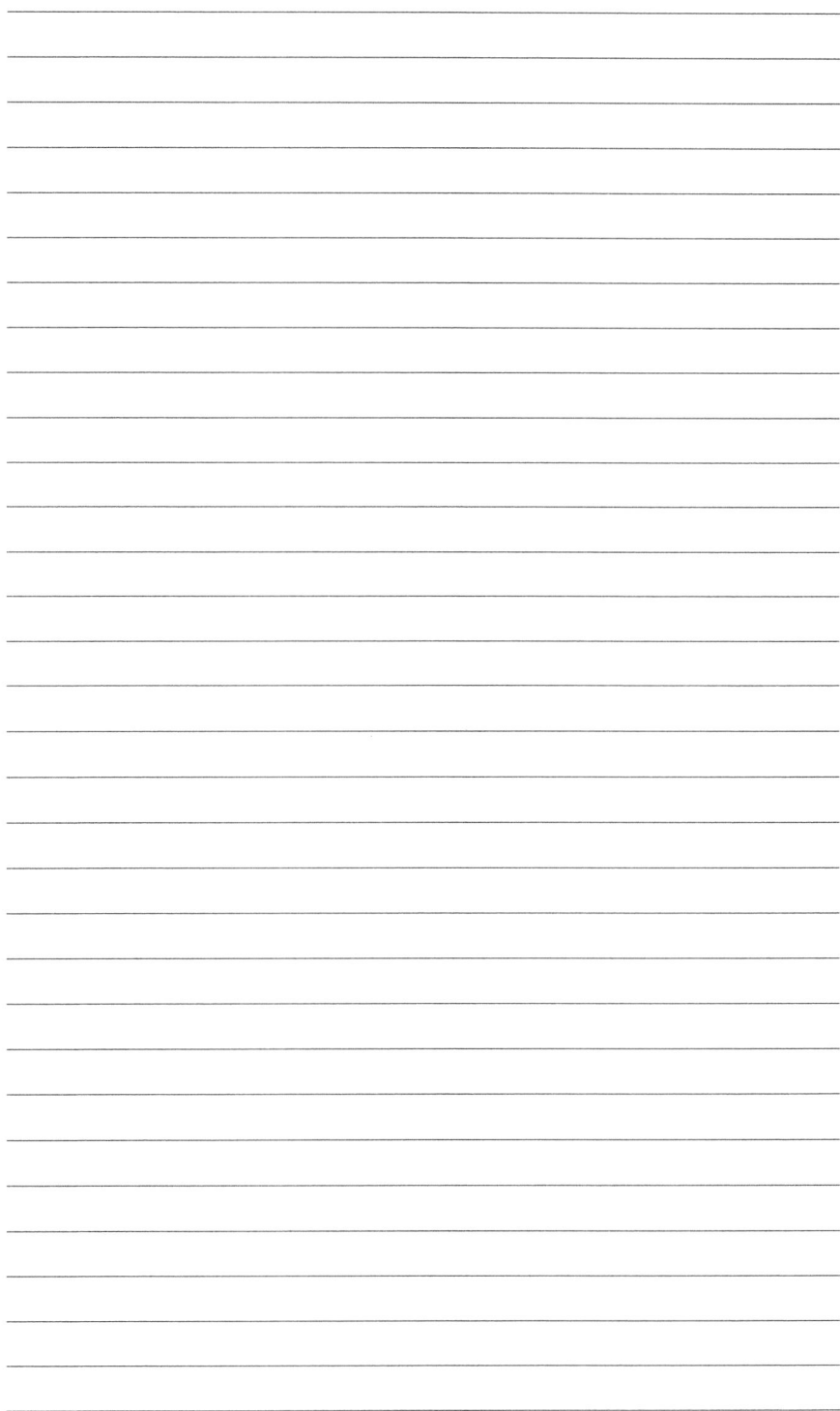

Thought for Day #23
Perfection is a myth. Today I will just be me.

Day #24 – *Imagine your body looks exactly the way you want it to. How do you imagine your life would change? In what ways is this realistic? In what ways is this unrealistic?*

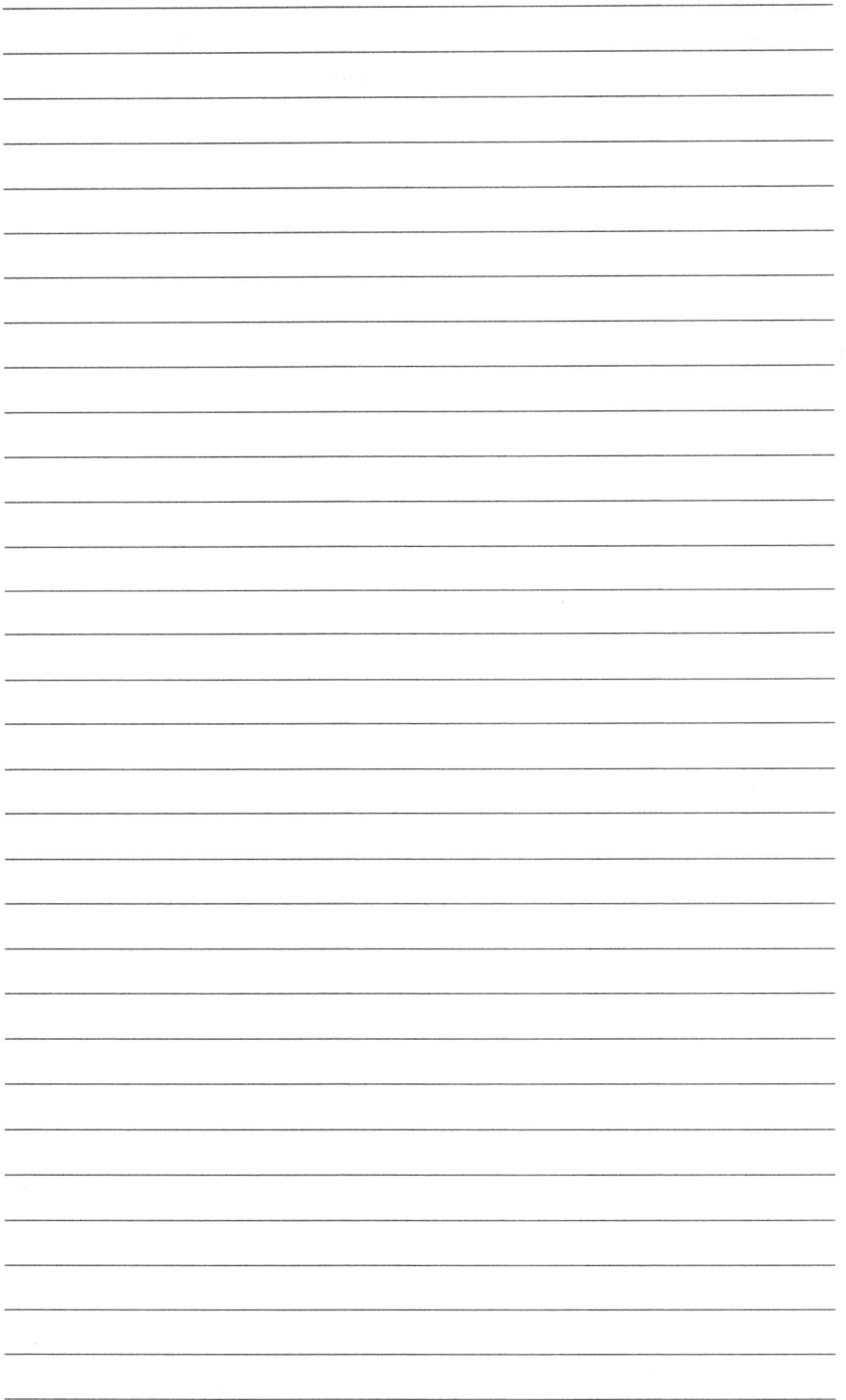

Thought for Day #24
Today I choose to appreciate myself as I am in this moment.

Day #25 – *Describe your experience of eating meals with other people.*
What parts of this experience do you enjoy?
What parts do you not enjoy?

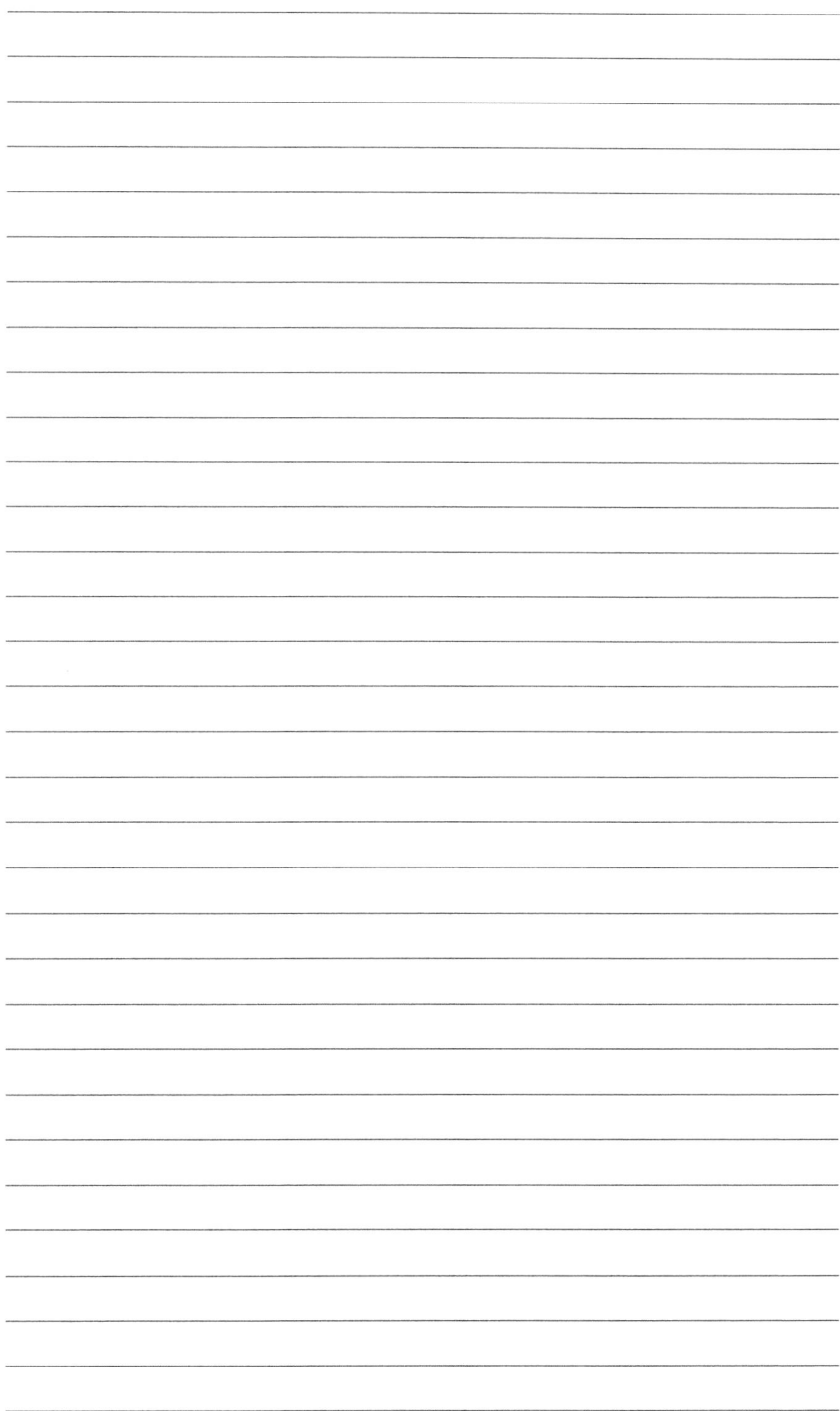

_____

_____

_____

_____

_____

_____

_____

_____

_____

_____

_____

_____

_____

_____

_____

_____

_____

_____

_____

_____

_____

_____

_____

_____ ๛

_____

Thought for Day #25
*I am worthy of being well-nourished at all times
and in all circumstances.*

Day #26 – *Describe your experience of shopping for clothing. Do you enjoy it? Do you avoid it? What is one thing you could do to make shopping for clothing a more enjoyable experience?*

✍

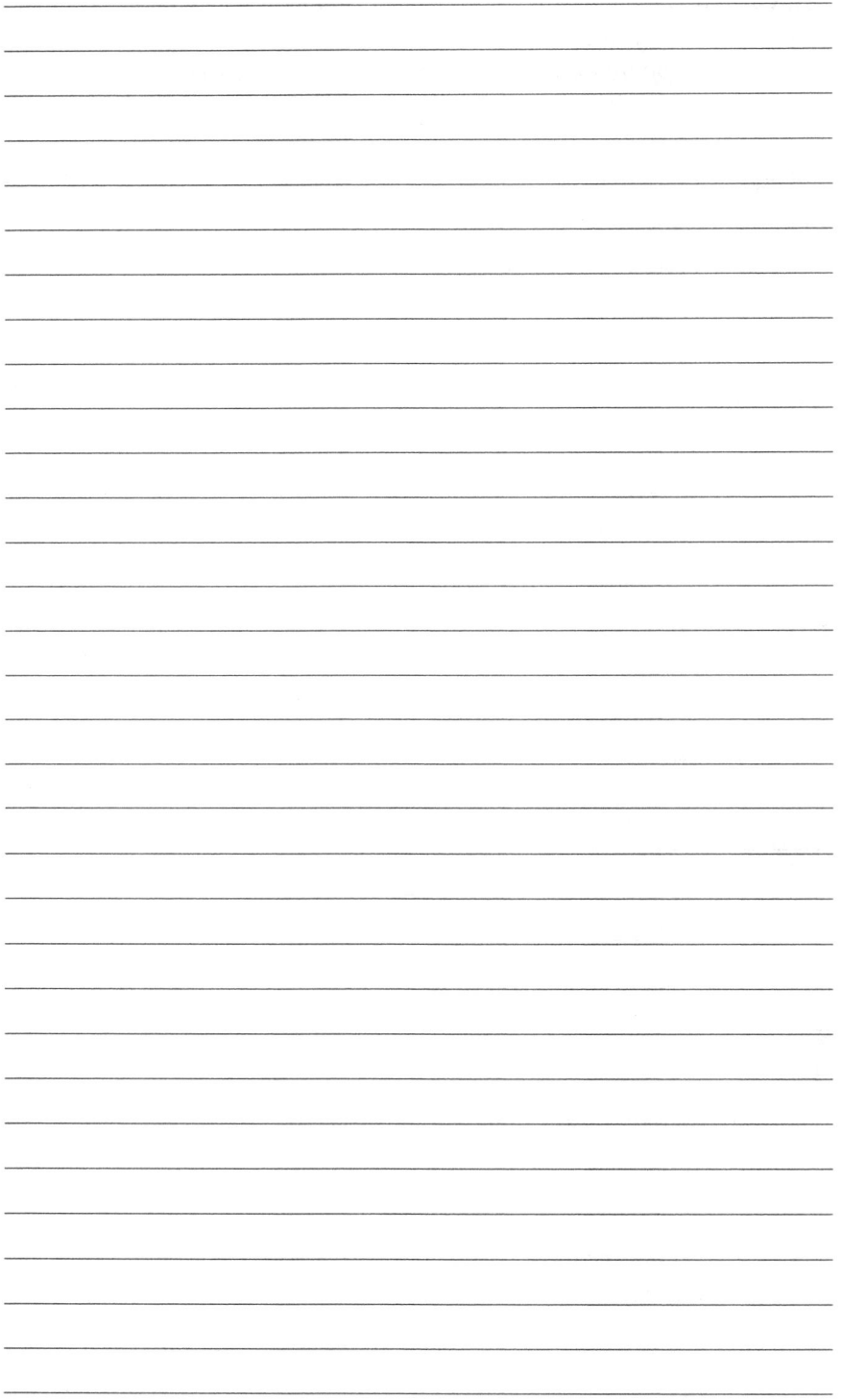

Thought for Day #26

I can be creative in coming up with new solutions to old problems!

Day #27 – *Describe your experience of shopping for food. Do you enjoy it? Do you avoid it? What is one thing you could do to make shopping for food more enjoyable?*

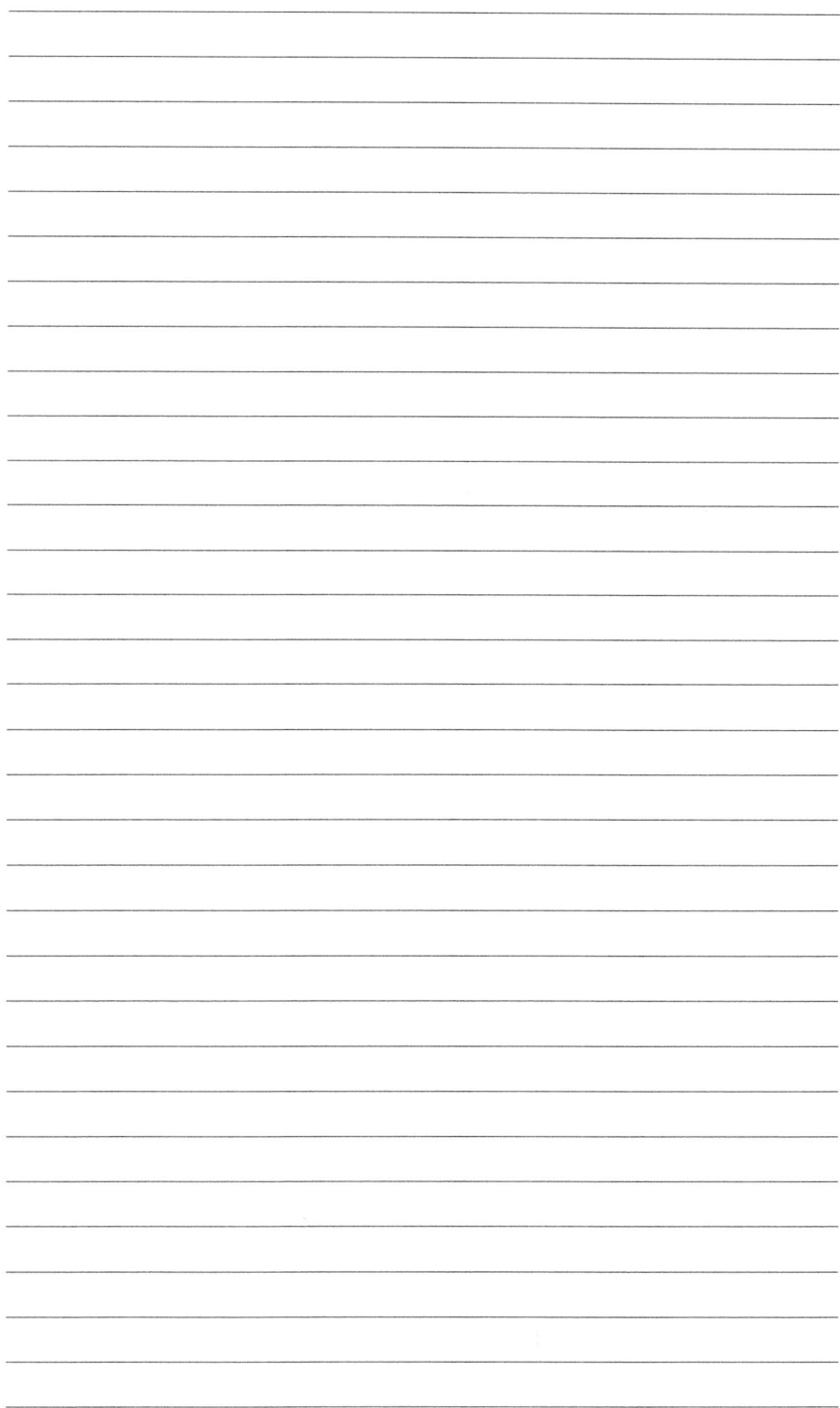

Thought for Day #27
I am worthy of nourishing and caring for myself.

Day #28 – *Describe your experience of preparing meals. Do you enjoy it? Do you avoid it? What is one thing you could do to make meal preparation more enjoyable?*

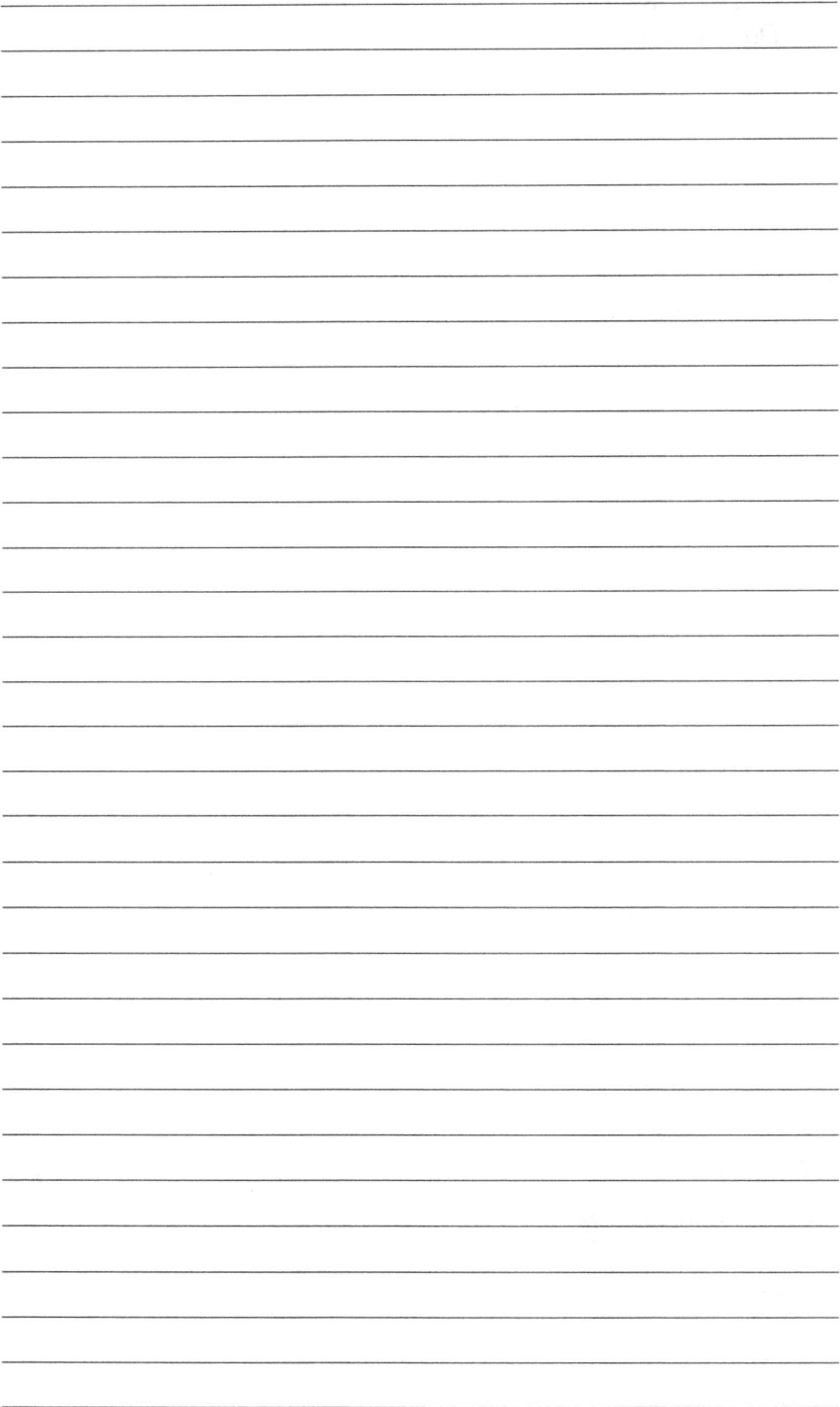

Thought for Day #28
I am capable of nourishing and caring for myself.

Day #29 – *How do you think your friends and family would respond to your losing weight?*

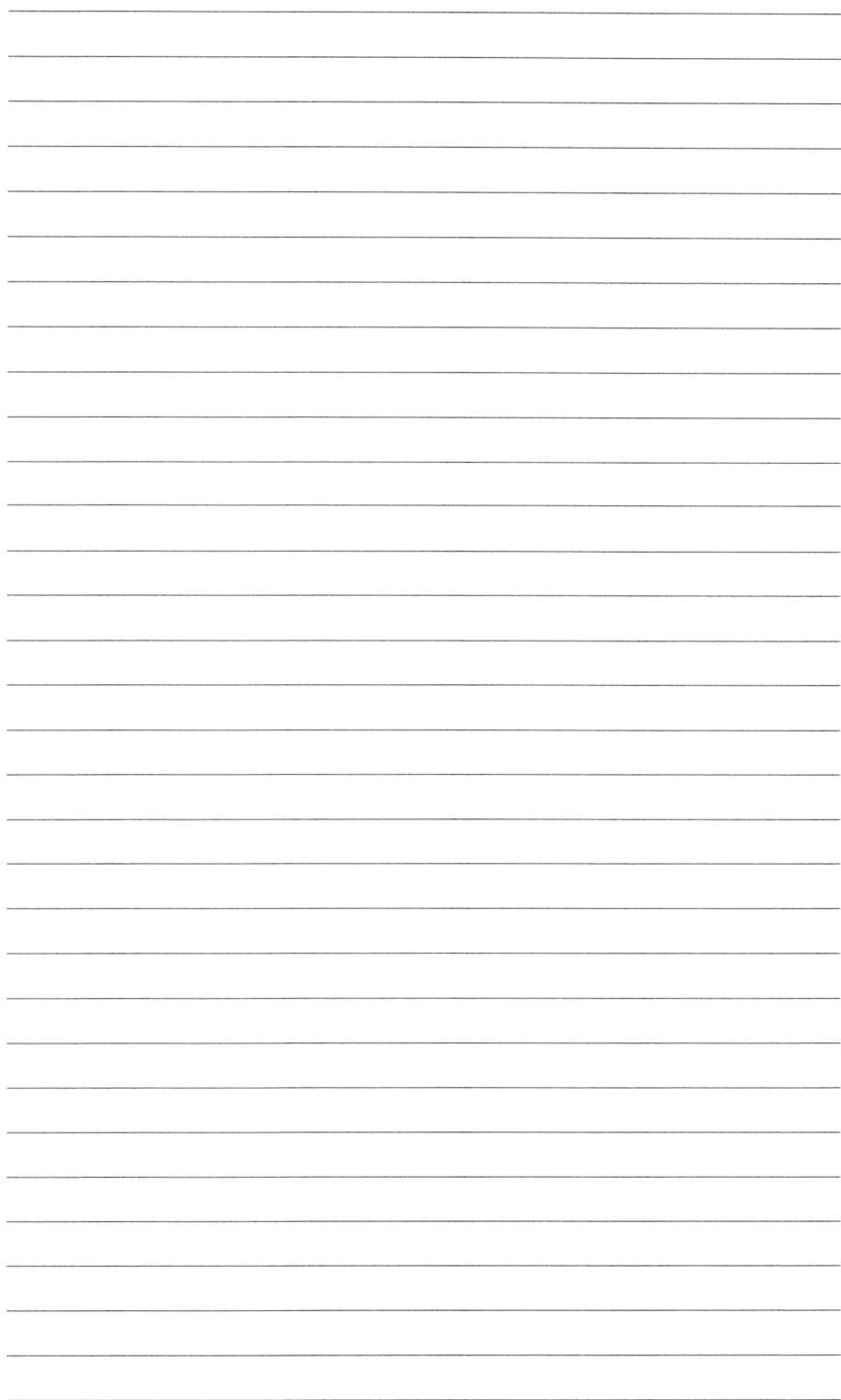

Thought for Day #29
It is loving to nurture and be kind to myself.

Day #30 – *What is something you can do to celebrate your body today, just as it is? When will you do it?*

❧

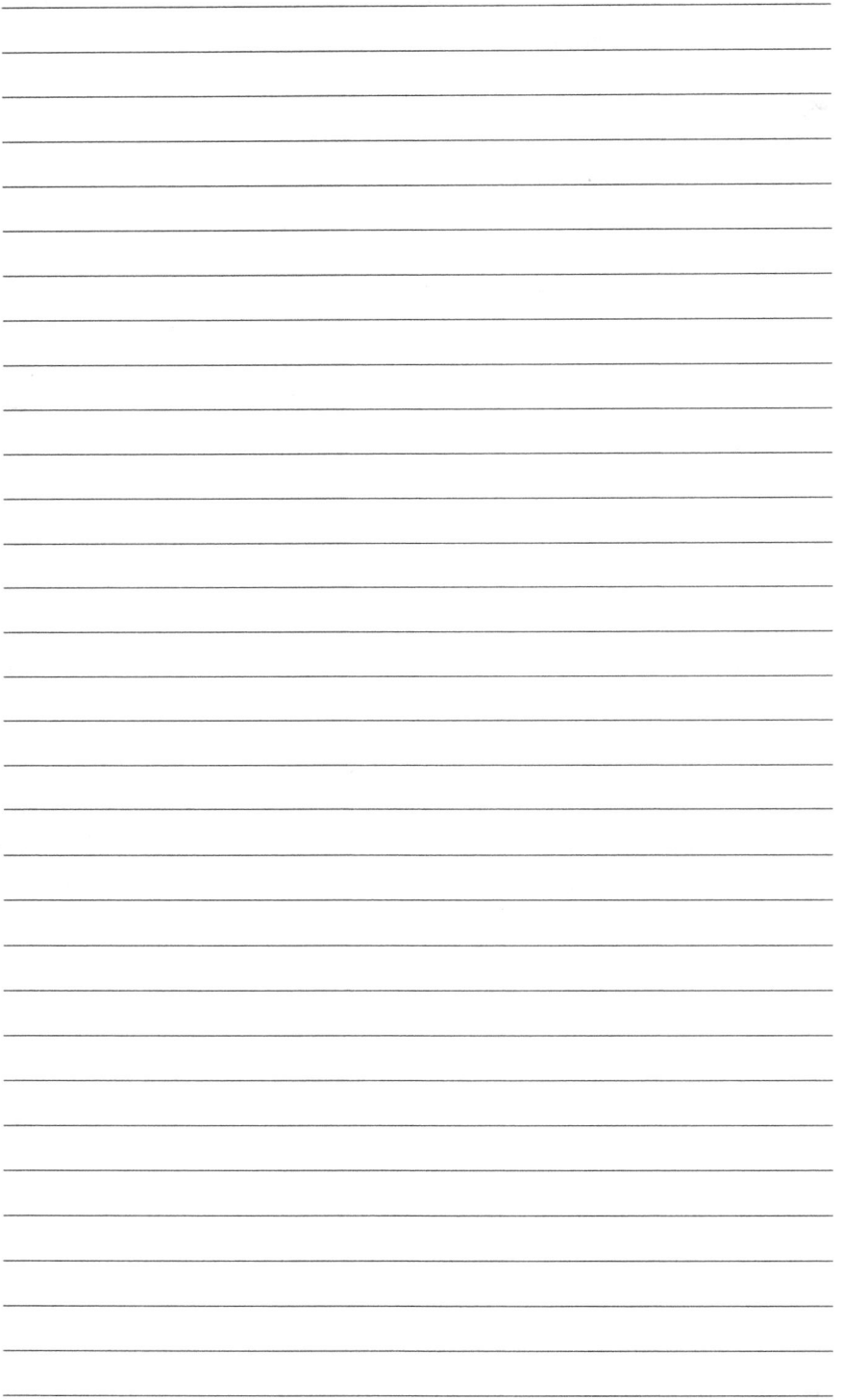

_____

_____

_____

_____

_____

_____

_____

_____

_____

_____

_____

_____

_____

_____

_____

_____

_____

_____

_____

_____

_____

_____

_____

_____

_____

_____

_____

ॐ

Thought for Day #30
*Today I will celebrate my body for the fact that however
I've treated it in the past, it keeps going!*

Day #31 – *When you see a thin, attractive stranger, what is your first thought about them? What do you believe other people think about you when you first meet them?*

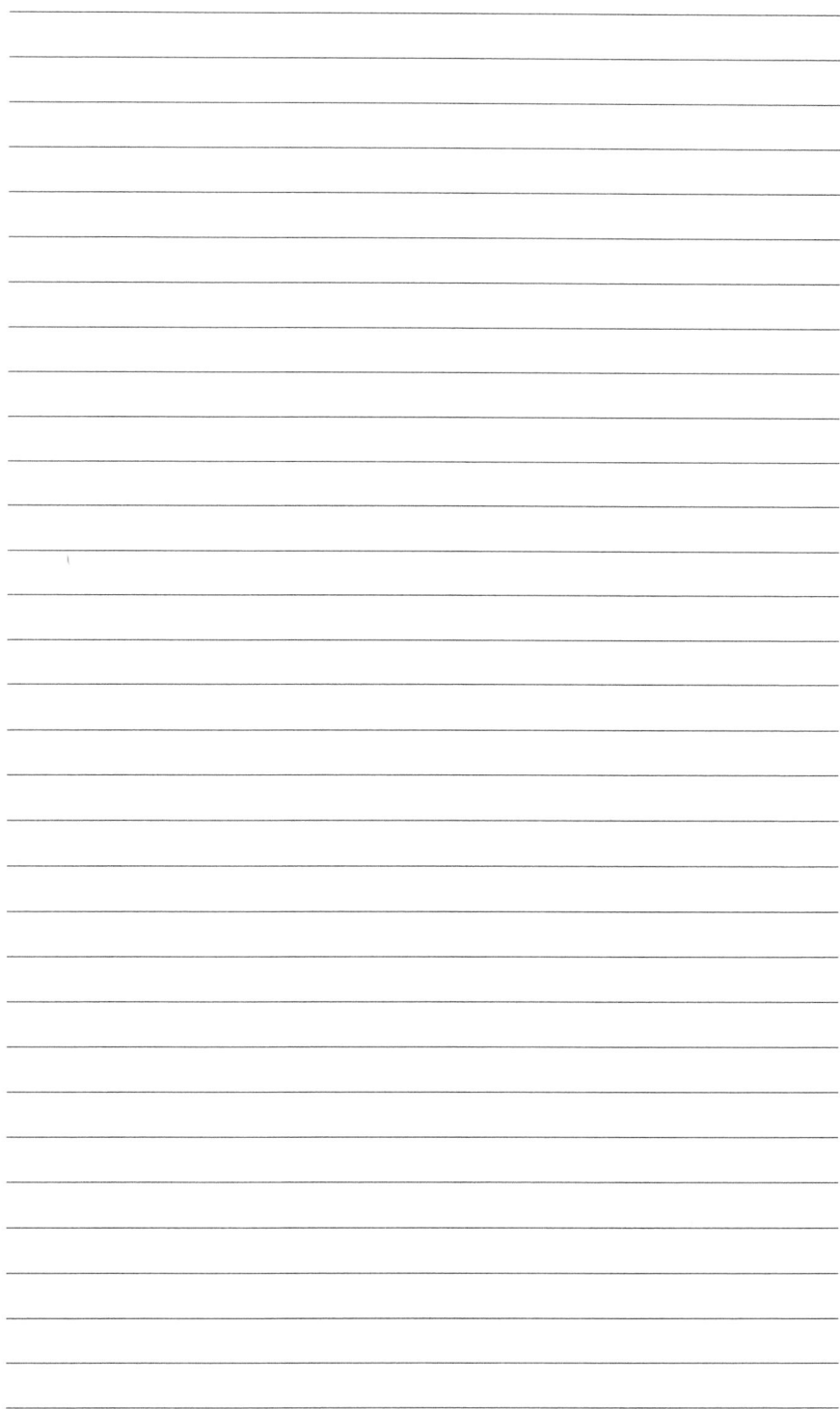

Thought for Day #31
Today I will remember that everyone has issues –
even thin, beautiful people!

Day #32 – *Finish this thought: "Because of my body, I don't…"*

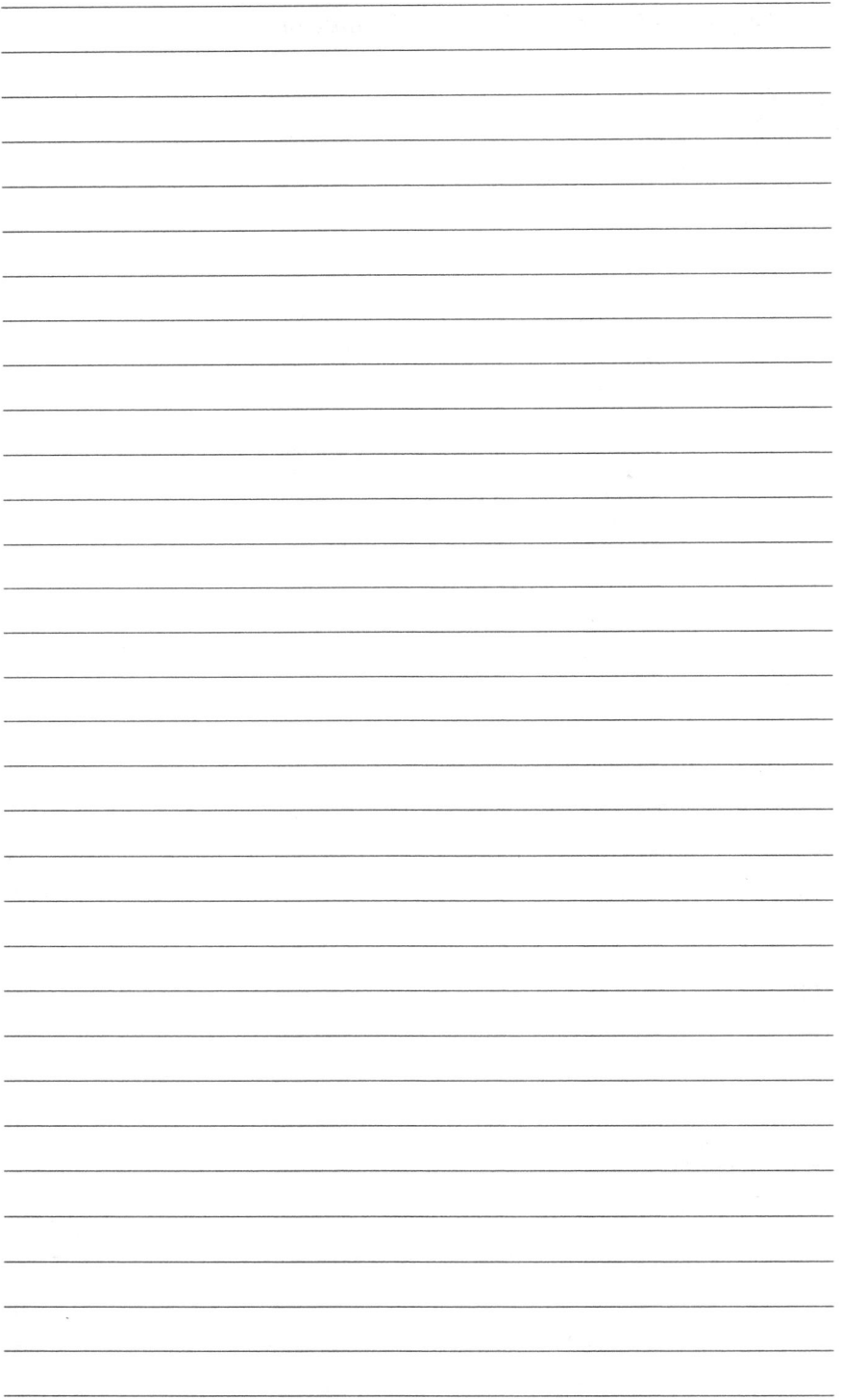

_____

_____

_____

_____

_____

_____

_____

_____

_____

_____

_____

_____

_____

_____

_____

_____

_____

_____

_____

_____

_____

_____

_____

_____

_____

_____

ഐ
_____

Thought for Day #32
Today, set a timer to go off once an hour. Each time it goes off,
write down one thing that you do well.

Day #33 – *Finish this thought: "Because of my body, I do…"*

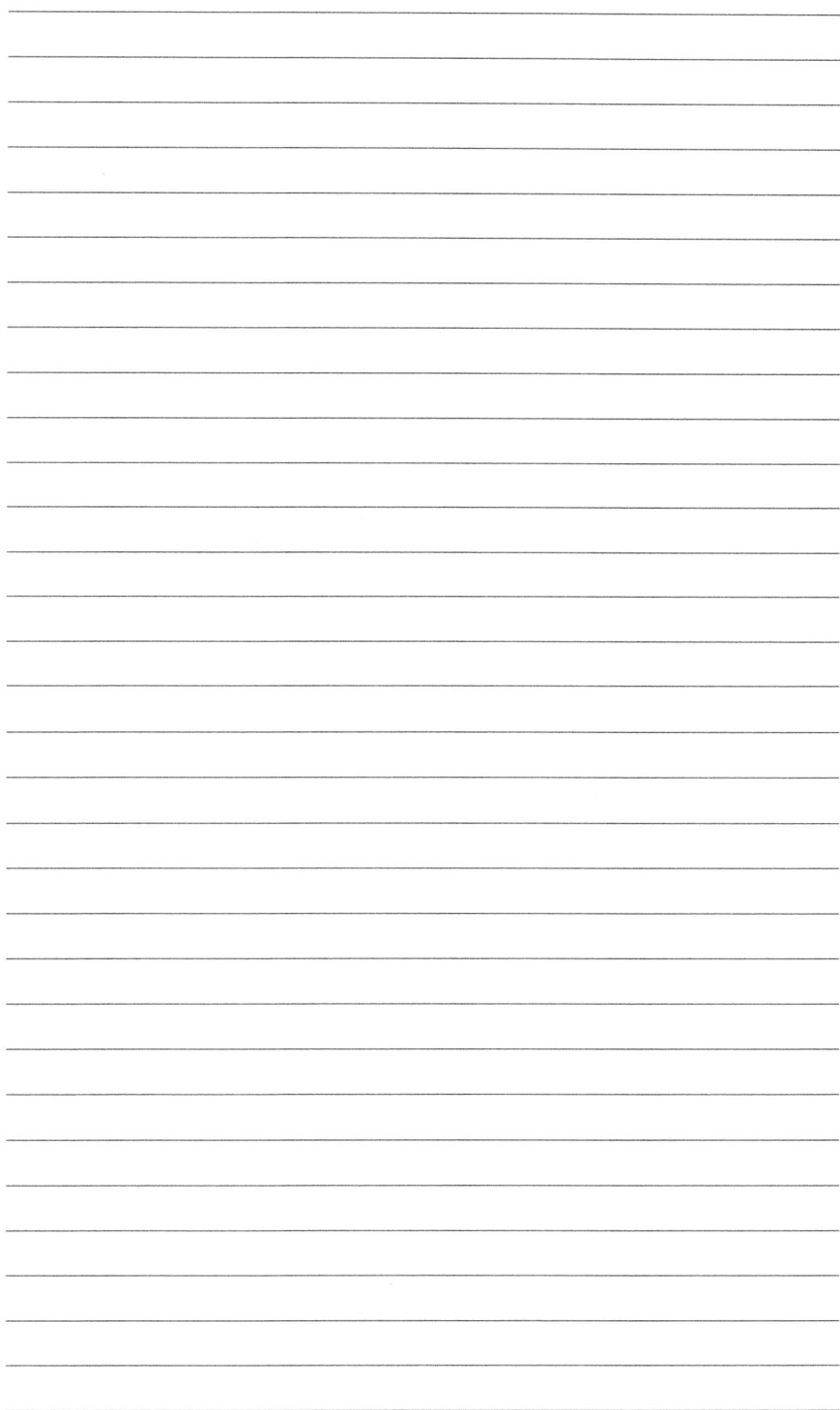

‰

Thought for Day #33
*Today, set a timer to go off once an hour. Each time it goes off,
write down one thing you appreciate about yourself.*

Day #34 – *Stand nude in front of a full-length mirror and look at yourself. YES! You CAN do this! Take a minute to listen to the voice(s) in your head. Write down what the voice(s) are saying. Whose voice(s) are they?*

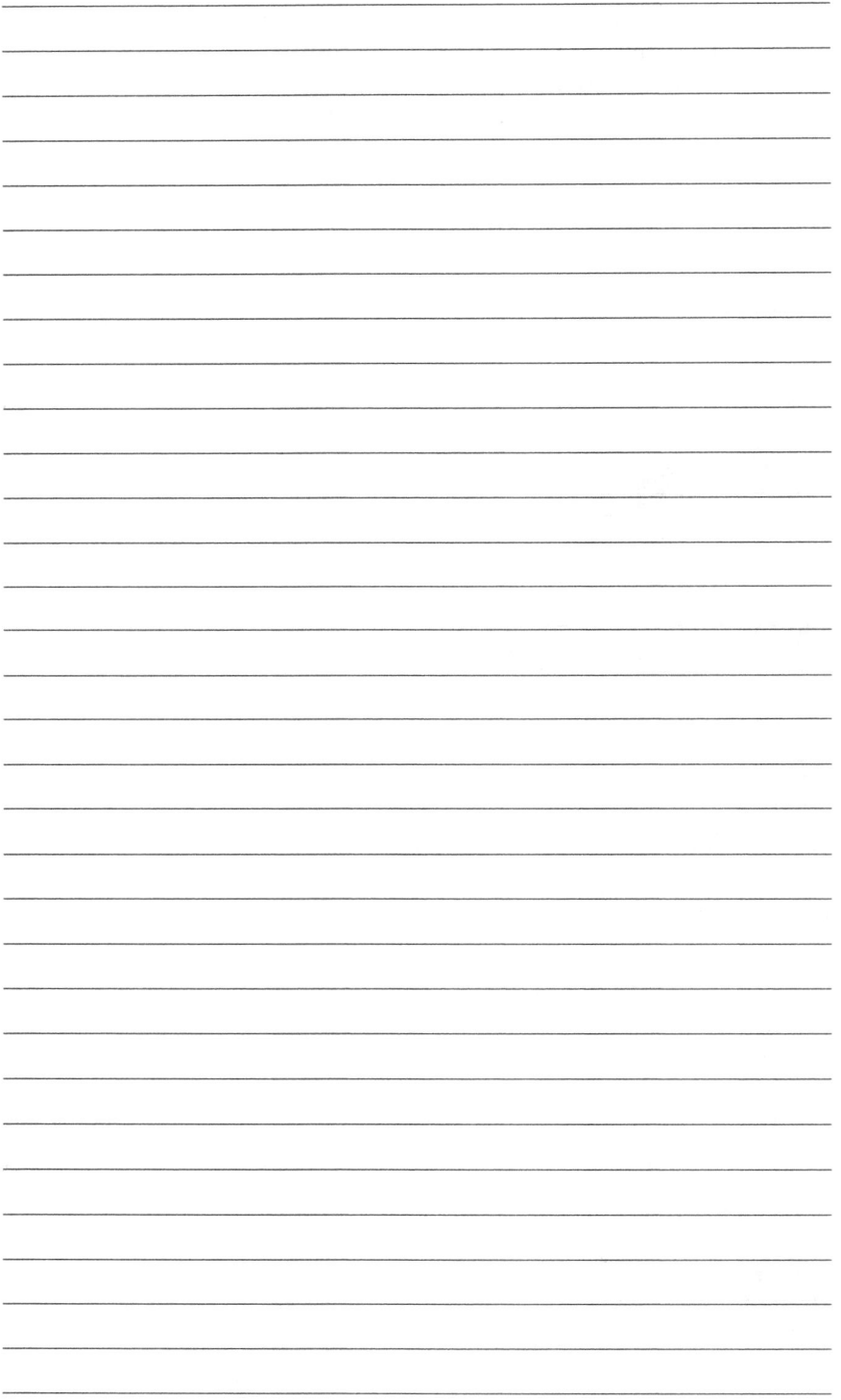

๛

Thought for Day #34
*Today I will pay attention to the voices in my head. When a voice
tells me something negative about myself, I will think about
whose voice it is and tell it to be quiet!*

Day #35 – *Are there things that you do for others that you don't take the time to do for yourself?*

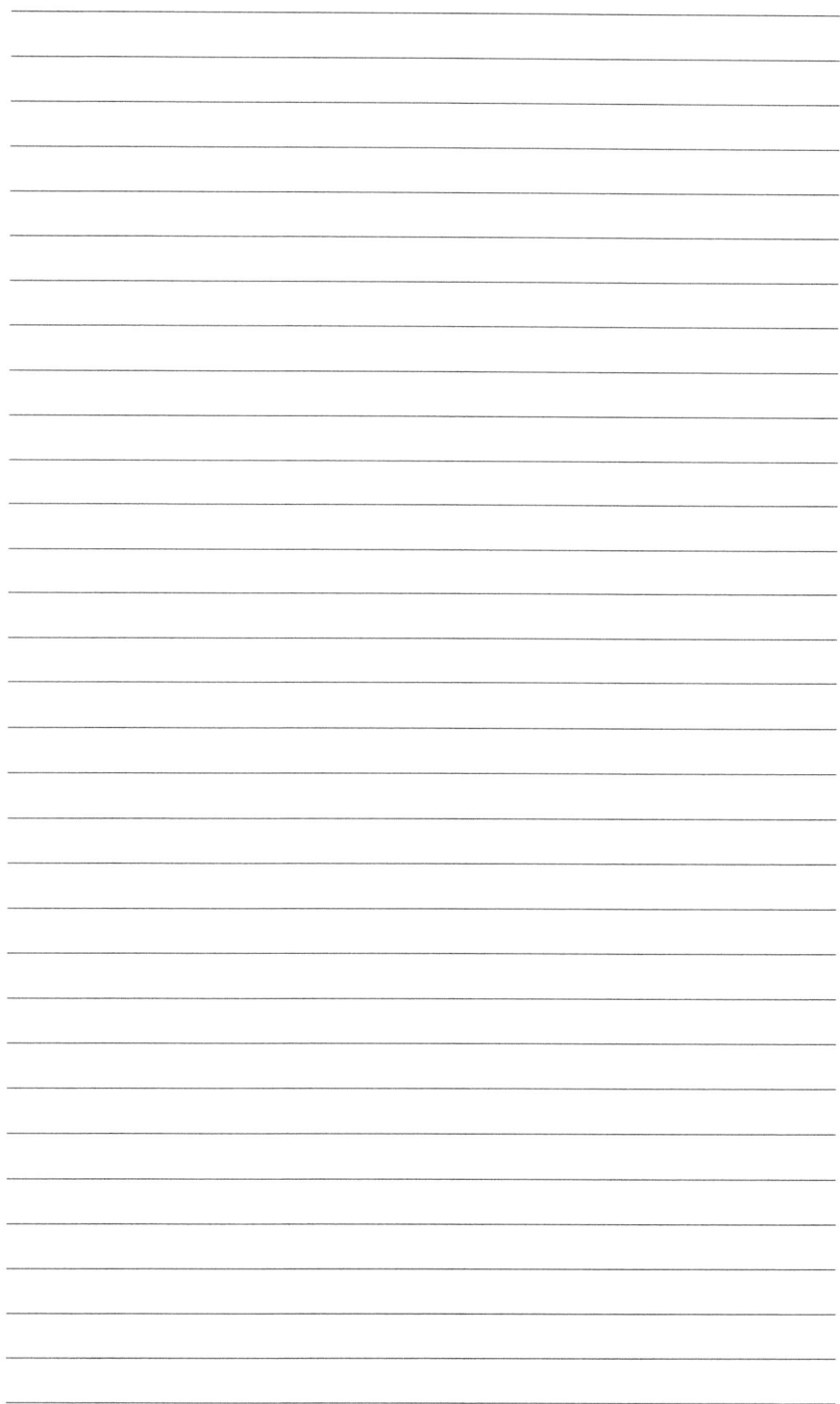

_____

_____

_____

_____

_____

_____

_____

_____

_____

_____

_____

_____

_____

_____

_____

_____

_____

_____

_____

_____

_____

_____

_____

_____

_____

ॐ
_____

Thought for Day #35
*Giving from an empty cup dishonors my body and spirit. Today I
choose to take care of myself so that I can give from the overflow.*

Day #36 – *How do you nourish yourself emotionally and spiritually? What is one small thing you can do to more fully nourish your mind and spirit?*

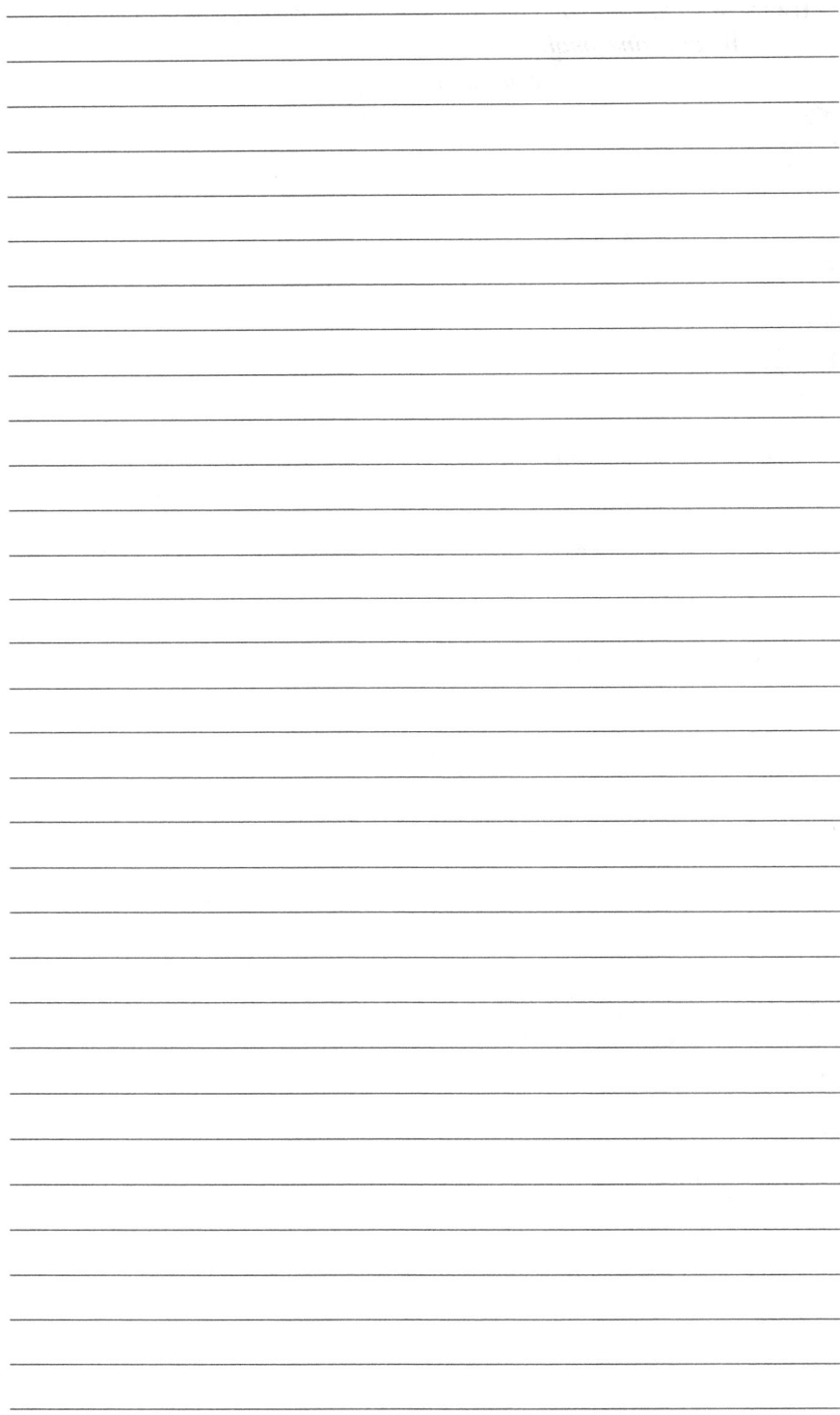

_____

_____

_____

_____

_____

_____

_____

_____

_____

_____

_____

_____

_____

_____

_____

_____

_____

_____

_____

_____

_____

_____

_____

_____

_____

_____

_____

ॐ

Thought for Day #36
*I am worthy of nourishing and caring for myself on all
levels – physically, mentally, emotionally, and spiritually.*

Day #37 – *Describe your current level of physical activity. What is one small change you can make to feel better about your current level of physical activity?*

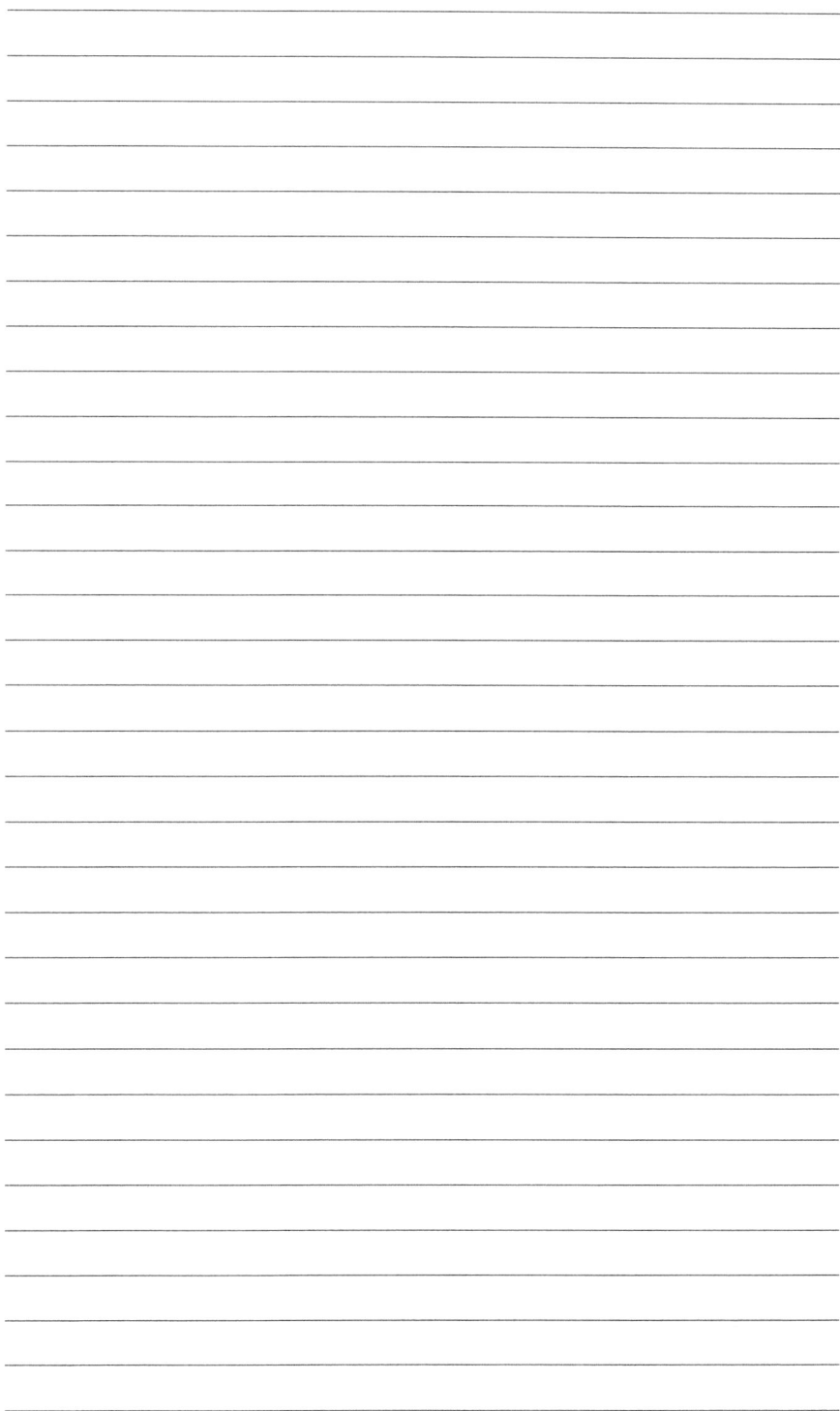

∽

Thought for Day #37
A healthy relationship with exercise begins with a healthy state of mind. My state of mind is getting better and better because I am willing to be good to myself!

Day #38 – *Describe your current way of eating.*
What is one small change you can make to feel
better about your current relationship with eating?

✍

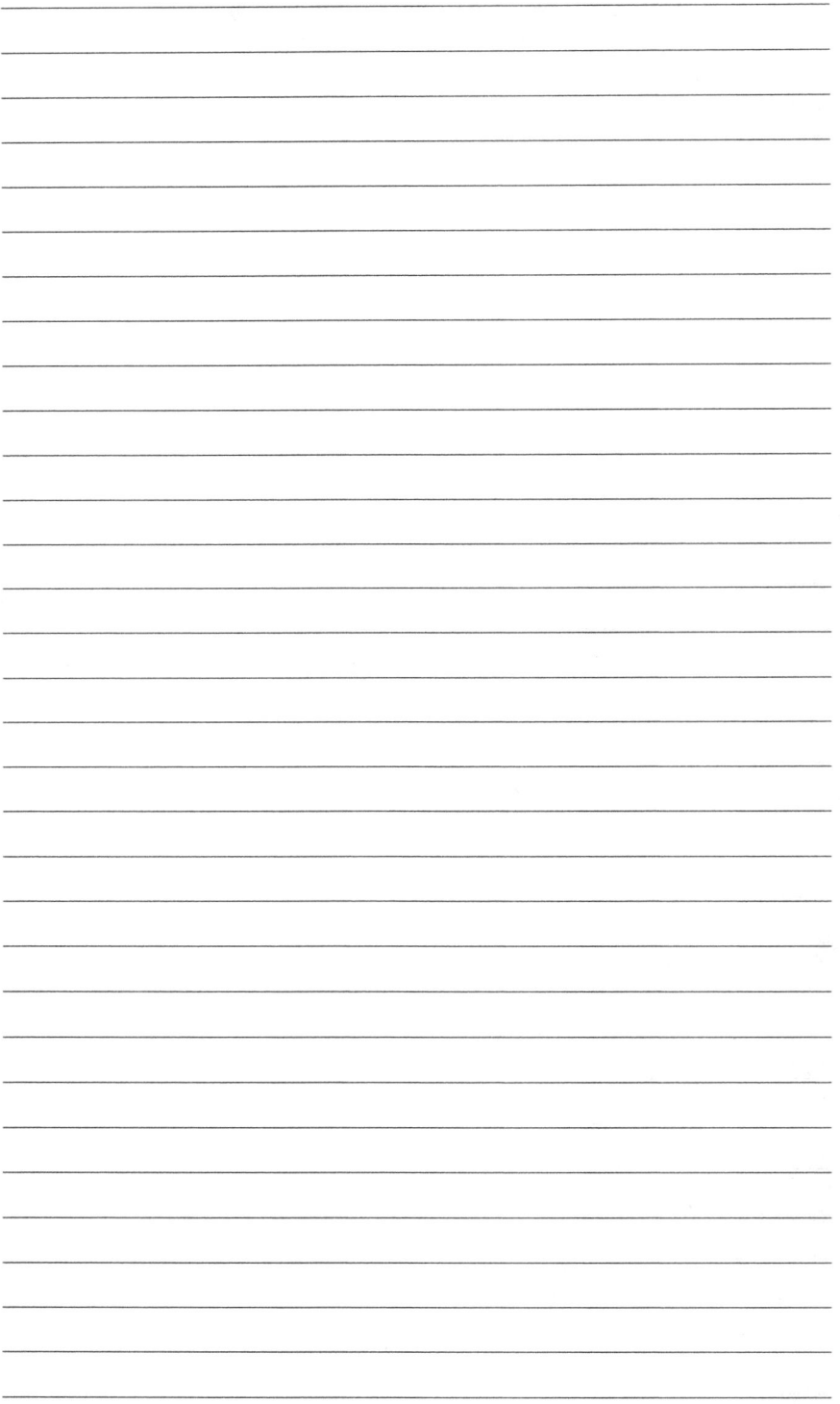

_____

_____

_____

_____

_____

_____

_____

_____

_____

_____

_____

_____

_____

_____

_____

_____

_____

_____

_____

_____

_____

_____

_____

_____

_____

_____

_____

_____

_____

_____

Thought for Day #38
Healthy eating begins with a healthy state of mind.
My state of mind is getting better and better because I
am willing to be good to myself!

Day #39 – *Think about a compliment you received recently. Did you believe the person? Write about why the compliment that person gave you is true.*

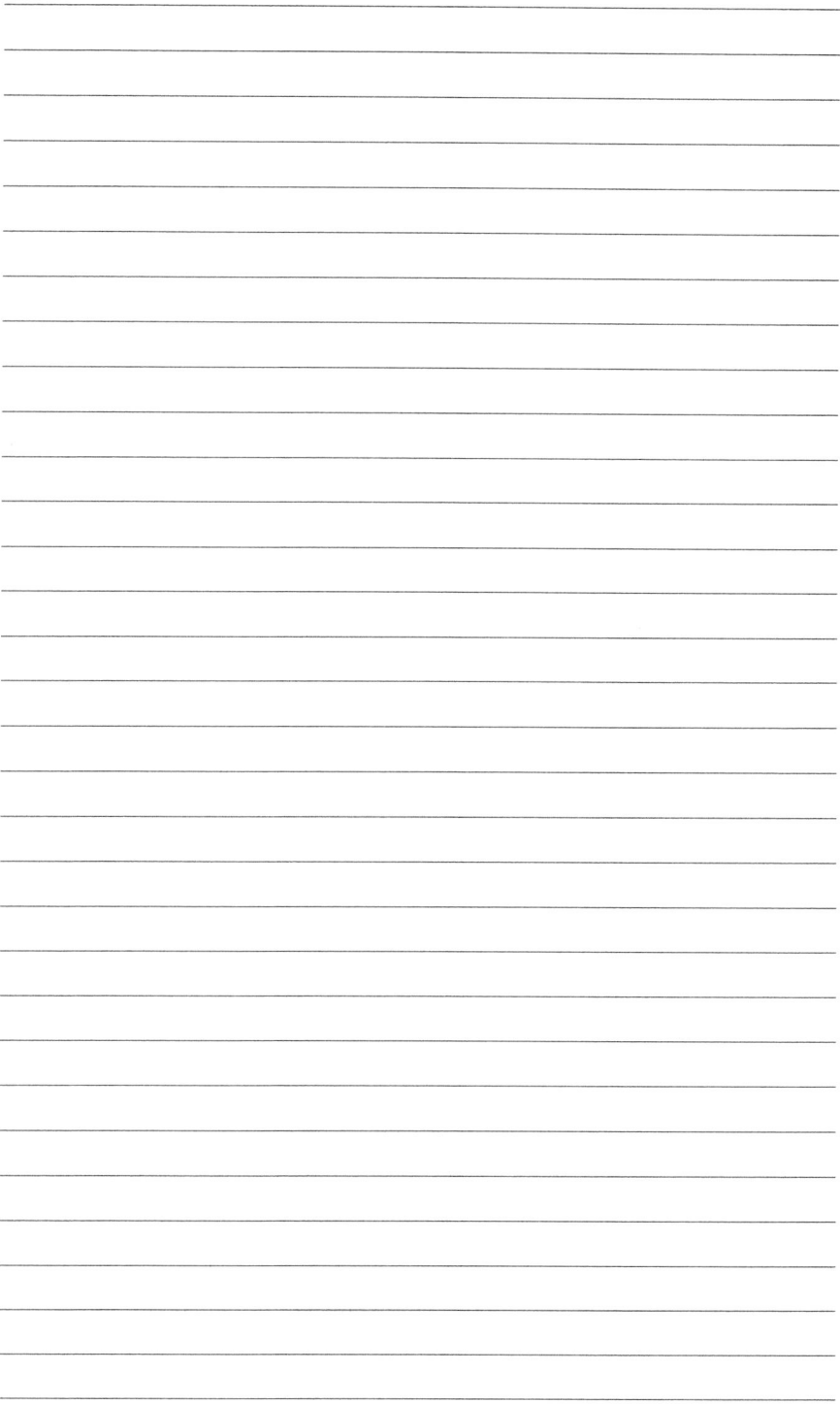

_____
_____
_____
_____
_____
_____
_____
_____
_____
_____
_____
_____
_____
_____
_____
_____
_____
_____
_____
_____
_____
_____
_____
_____
_____
_____
_____

Thought for Day #39

*There is a difference between acknowledging my goodness
and being conceited. Today, I will practice acknowledging
the things that I do well.*

Day #40 – *Reflect on how you felt about your weight and your body when you began Day #1 of this process. How have your thoughts and attitudes changed since you began?*

ೋ

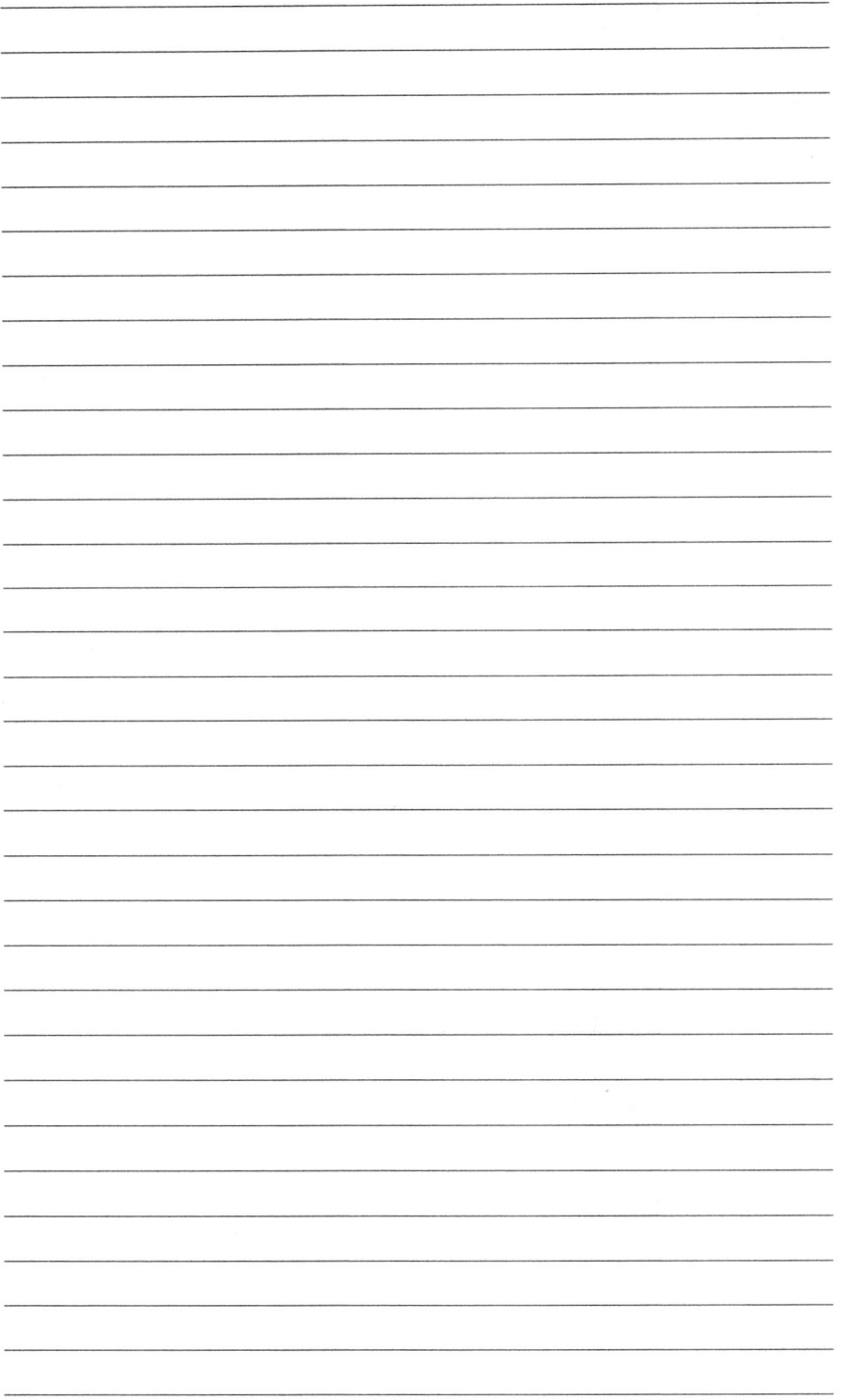

_____

_____

_____

_____

_____

_____

_____

_____

_____

_____

_____

_____

_____

_____

_____

_____

_____

_____

_____

_____

_____

_____

_____

_____

_____

_____

_____

_____

Thought for Day #40
*Today I honor and appreciate myself for completing
something that helps me to take care of me.*
I AM WORTHY!!!!

ABOUT LEAH

Leah Carey is a journalist for a daily newspaper in Vermont where she specializes in human interest features.

She is also the **Chief Miracle Officer** for *The Miracle Journal*, where she details the large and small miracles that happen in her life every day. She encourages readers to send in their own stories of everyday miracles. You can find *The Miracle Journal* at www. TheMiracleJournal.com.

As a speaker and teacher, Leah shares universal principles in practical ways so you can integrate them into your daily life. She specializes in down-to-earth solutions for everyday issues.

Her philosophy is that it's not about fixing who you are or what you do. It's about figuring out what's already right in your life and building from there.

To learn more, visit *www.TheMiracleJournal.com*
or *www.LeahCarey.com*.

Want more tips for how to live an inspired and joyful life? Sign up for Leah's weekly newsletter at http://tinyurl.com/miraclejournal.